# LEGATO&TAPPING
# ROCKGUITARETUDES

Master Fluid Legato & Tapping Techniques for Faster, More Dynamic Guitar Solos

## SHAUNBAXTER

FUNDAMENTAL**CHANGES**

# Legato & Tapping Rock Guitar Etudes

**Master Fluid Legato & Tapping Techniques for Faster, More Dynamic Guitar Solos**

ISBN: 978-1-78933-458-6

Published by **www.fundamental-changes.com**

Copyright © 2024 Shaun Baxter

Edited by Joseph Alexander and Tim Pettingale

**www.fundamental-changes.com**

Join our free Facebook Community of Cool Musicians

**www.facebook.com/groups/fundamentalguitar**

Instagram: **FundamentalChanges**

For over 350 Free Guitar Lessons with Videos Check Out

**www.fundamental-changes.com**

Cover Image Copyright: Shaun Baxter

All etudes audio recorded and mixed at W. M. Studios by Phil Hilborne

All short music examples audio recorded and mixed at Brakenhurst Studios by Shaun Baxter

All transcriptions by Shaun Baxter

# Contents

# About the Author

Shaun Baxter was a founder member of The Guitar Institute in London in 1986 (which was partnered with the London College of Music and became the biggest trade-school for guitar in Europe) where he taught every week for over 20 years. He went on to be Head of Guitar at Guitar-X in London before, in 2003, becoming an owner and the Academic Director of The Academy of Music and Sound (AMS), a national network of music schools with centres all over the UK. At one point, via their various apprenticeship schemes, AMS were the biggest employer in the Scottish music industry and their alumni includes Lewis Capaldi.

Shaun composed the world's first Grade 8 Guitar syllabus for Trinity College, wrote the UK's National Operational Standards (NOS) for music performance, and contributed to magazines such as *The Guitar Magazine*, *Guitar World*, *Metal Hammer* and *Guitar Techniques* (for whom he wrote a popular and influential monthly column for 27 years).

Through his teaching, Shaun helped to pioneer popular music education in the UK and taught many high profile guitarists such as Rick Graham, Andy James, Jon Gomm and Justin Sandercoe, as well as many others who have found fame with artists such as Public Image Ltd, Asia, Craig David, Moby, Wynton Marsalis, Haken, Martin Taylor, Steve Hackett, Rick Wakeman, Mike Oldfield, The Art of Noise, Leo Sayer, Pet Shop Boys, Roger Waters and Queen.

During the '90s, he was a member of the Composition Department at the London College of Music and also lectured at Brunel University, Leeds College of Music, University of West London, Bath Spa University, Coventry University and Rostock University of Music and Drama in Germany.

In 1993, Shaun recorded his ground-breaking *Jazz Metal* solo album.

He has performed with players such as Uli Jon Roth (Scorpions), Neil Murray (Whitesnake, Black Sabbath), and Ron "Bumblefoot" Thal (Guns & Roses), and also toured the world and/or recorded with artists such as Princess, John Sloman (Gary Moore/Uriah Heep), Todd Rundgren and Carl Palmer of Emerson Lake and Palmer.

*"He is one of the greatest musicians I have played with."* (Carl Palmer, legendary progressive rock drummer).

As an artist, he has been an official endorsee of Marshall Amplification, Cornford Amplification, Fender Guitars, Patrick Eggle Guitars, Line 6 effects, Two-Note Audio Engineering, and Picato Strings.

Shaun was one of only eight heavy metal guitar players (along with Edward Van Halen, Joe Satriani, Steve Vai, Yngwie Malmsteen, Nuno Bettencourt, Michael Schenker and Paul Gilbert) featured in the world's biggest-selling music book, *Guitar: A Complete Guide for the Player* (2002).

He appeared in a list of "the top 50 rock guitar players since the 1980s" in *Guitarist* magazine and was also included in *The Guitarist's Book of Guitarist Players* (1994) which details "the world's most influential guitarists and bass players". His album, *Jazz Metal* topped its 50 recommended fusion guitar recordings.

Shaun is the bestselling author of the guitar methods:

- *Chromatic Lead Guitar Techniques*
- *Dominant Pentatonic Scale Guitar Soloing*
- *Creative Intervallic Guitar Soloing*

All published by **www.Fundamental-Changes.com**

# Introduction

## What is Legato?

In music, "legato" means *smooth* and *tied together*. In rock guitar, this refers to playing most notes using a mixture of hammer-ons and pull-offs, where only the first note on each string is picked. This technique creates the continuous, flowing sound heard in the playing of guitarists like Allan Holdsworth, Brett Garsed, and Joe Satriani.

## Why is it Important?

There are far more pages in guitar magazines dedicated to the picking hand than the fretting hand. However, while it's possible to be a great guitarist with a less-developed picking hand, it's impossible to be one with a poor fretting hand. Because of this, developing your fretting hand should be your top priority.

Many guitarists underestimate how much legato is used in modern rock and often lack the fretting-hand discipline needed to play controlled lines and sequences at an even tempo. This leads them to pick far more notes than they need to emulate some of their favourite guitarists.

It's also easier to play at high speed using legato and tapping, as a pull-off allows you to sound a note when your finger leaves the fretboard.

At fast tempos, legato tends to sound more articulate than picking. This is because picking a string creates an audible "click" or transient frequency, and when picking a rapid series of notes, the pitch of each note barely has time to settle after the transient before you move to the next one. Legato playing avoids that initial click, allowing the note's pitch to ring out fully so that you can hear it clearly at any speed.

## What is an Etude?

*Etudes* are short musical compositions designed to improve your technique and showcase your skills. As such, they are an efficient way to cover a wide range of disciplines in a short amount of time, and are great for building stamina. In my teaching career, I've noticed that students normally prefer playing study pieces rather than working through hundreds of exercises.

For each etude, rather than aiming to create a beautiful piece of music, I simply compiled a long list of exercises that are effective for mastering a specific technique then combined them in the most straightforward way. These are intended as technical studies, not artistic musical statements.

Don't worry, these etudes won't turn you into a neo-classical metal player. Think of them as efficient technical workouts that are both rhythmically and melodically simple, allowing you to focus on developing your technique and stamina.

## Avoiding Repetitive Strain Injury (RSI)

When focusing on a single technique, RSI can be a legitimate concern. To avoid it, the first rule is to keep your practice sessions short and regular.

Players who have suffered repetitive strain injuries say that they are often fine when they are improvising but their symptoms return as soon as they start playing the same thing repeatedly. Repetition does feature as part of learning, but it should take the form of a short daily reminder for the brain to absorb something, rather than a 5-hour stint once a week. For this reason, avoid too much repetition of the same movement.

Never continue through pain, and as soon as you get any kind of twinge, stop! There are always loads of other things to practice that will not be so physically demanding, so get on with that until you feel it's safe for you to resume. After a while, you should be able to distinguish between the warm feeling of a healthy workout and the sort of discomfort that may be an indication that you are overdoing it. Your stamina will increase as you go along, so be patient and give it time to develop. If in doubt, see a specialist doctor.

## Posture

Posture is important when you play, but don't confuse good posture with the preconception of the "rigid" classical musician. We can have good posture and still look like a rock star! These tips are a good starting point:

- Make sure that your shoulders don't rise when you play. This will lead to chronic tension, which could create serious problems (often elsewhere) if continued

- Your elbows should hang loosely by your sides, not held aloft or tight to your body

- Practice standing up, not sitting down

- If reading from a chart set it at head height so that you don't have to constantly look down

- Don't have your guitar slung too low. Ideally, the guitar body should lie across the middle of your stomach

# Get the Audio

The audio files for this book are available to download for free from **www.fundamental-changes.com.** The link is in the top right-hand corner. Click on the "Guitar" link then simply select this book title from the drop-down menu and follow the instructions to get the audio.

We recommend that you download the files directly to your computer, not to your tablet, and extract them there before adding them to your media library. You can then put them onto your tablet, iPod or burn them to CD. On the download page there are instructions and we also provide technical support via the contact form.

For over 350 free guitar lessons with videos check out:

**www.fundamental-changes.com**

Join our free Facebook Community of Cool Musicians

**www.facebook.com/groups/fundamentalguitar**

Tag us for a share on Instagram: **FundamentalChanges**

# Chapter One: Basic Legato Technique

A key consideration affecting all aspects of playing electric guitar is eliminating unwanted noise from the strings, which is often more apparent when playing with distortion. This noise becomes especially important with legato playing, as having less "attack" makes the notes less able to compete with background noise.

To play cleanly with distortion, it's essential to examine how each hand functions and adapt them to keep unwanted noise to a minimum.

# The Picking Hand

Although legato focuses mainly on the fretting hand, the picking hand also plays its part in keeping everything clean. Its main roll here is to damp idle bass strings.

## Damping Idle Bass Strings with the Picking Hand

*Damping* is the practice of resting the side of the picking hand (karate-chop style) firmly on any unused strings below the string being played. This stops the strings from vibrating altogether and eradicates idle open bass string noise.

**Photo 1**

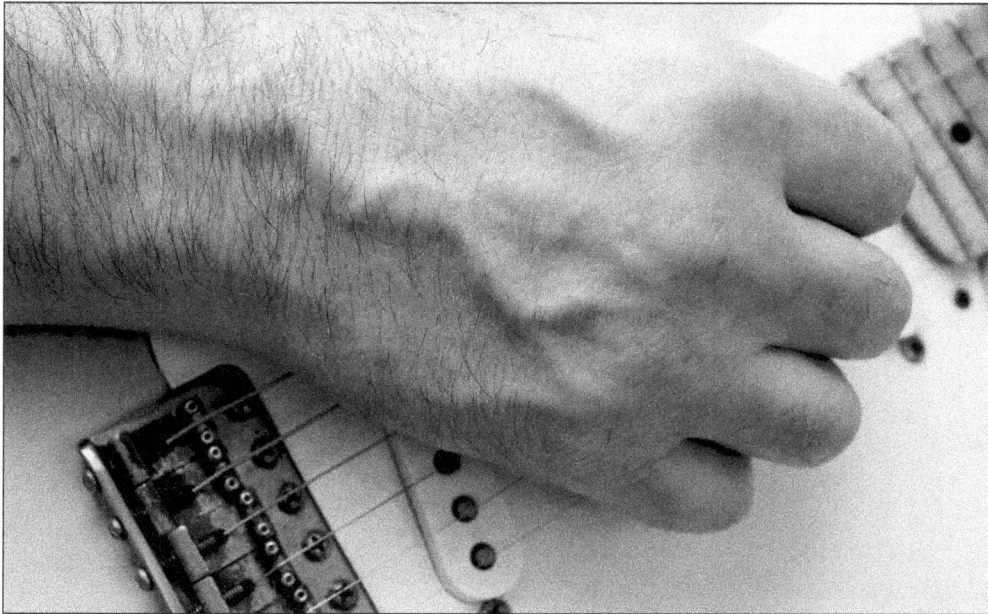

Check there is a visible gap between your hand and the bridge. If you rest your hand *on* the bridge, the open bass strings will vibrate because they will only be muted (reduced vibration) rather than damped (no vibration).

Karate chopping the idle bass strings requires you to reach out towards the strings more with the pick held by the thumb and finger(s) than you may be used to. The profile of the knuckle of your first finger should be high, with an "O" shaped hole formed by your thumb and first finger.

**Photo 2**

## Transition of Picking Hand from Bass String to Treble Strings

To maintain a consistent picking action when playing the low E string, you must rest on the guitar body with the side of the hand.

**Photo 3**

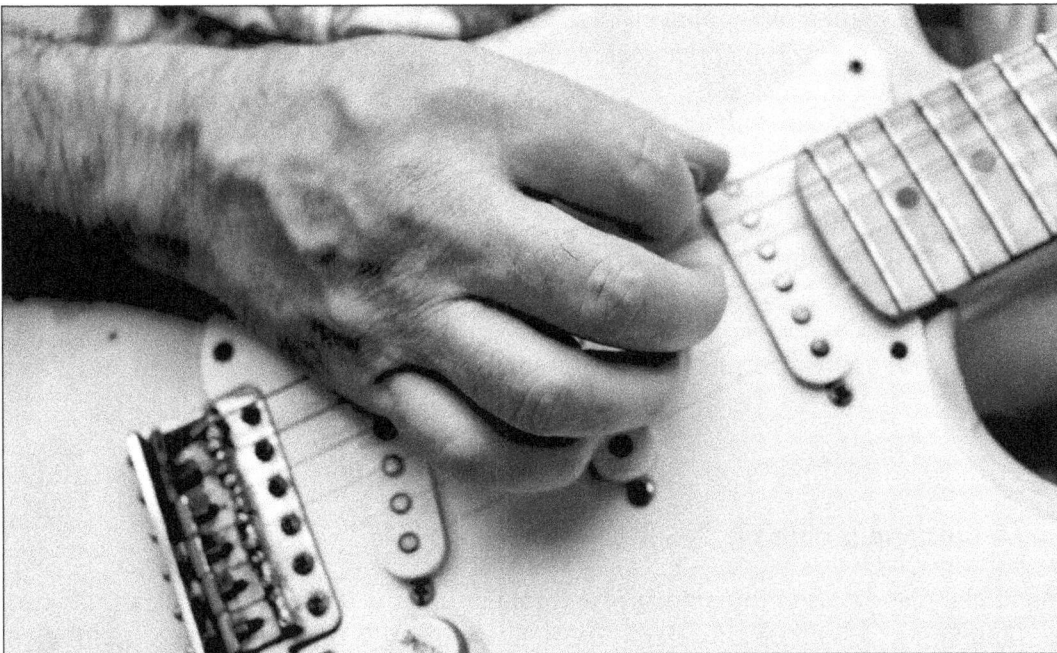

It is important *not* to raise your shoulder to keep the wrist straight – you need to bend the wrist instead. After a while this position will start to feel comfortable. Do not rest your fingers on the scratch-plate.

## Contact with Side of Thumb

If you show as little of the pick to the string as possible, extra damping will come from the side of the thumb as it rests on the unused bass string immediately below the one you are picking. For example, if picking the G string, the side of your thumb should rub back and forth on the D string.

**Photo 4**

This may feel odd at first but, like everything else, you'll get used to it after a while. If isolated, it does produce a slight swishing noise, but this will be unnoticeable beneath the volume of your picked notes.

It is a technique that has several advantages:

- By always rubbing/resting on it with the thumb, an adjacent bass string will prevent you from pushing too much pick into the plane of the string, which can result in you hitting a "snag" when picking at high speed. In other words, the thumb acts as a depth gauge, resulting in a very precise and consistent amount of pick being applied to the string each time.

- It provides you with a physical reference point, allowing you to always feel where the strings are, thus aiding accuracy.

## Damping Idle Treble Strings with the Picking Hand

The picking hand can also be used to dampen idle treble strings by resting the back of the curled-up fourth finger on them. This finger should be closed into the hand along with the third and second fingers.

**Photo 5**

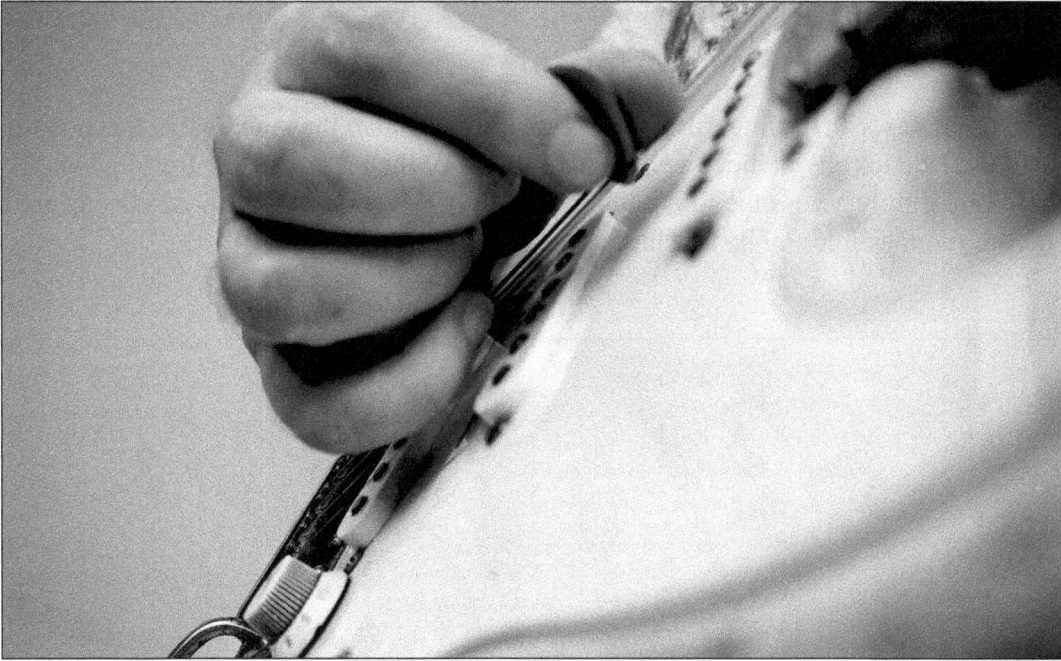

## Damping Treble Strings with the Fretting Hand

In rock guitar, we fret notes with the fingerprint part of the fingers rather than the tips. In this position any unused higher strings should be naturally damped with the underside of the fingers of the fretting hand (especially the first, which should lie lightly across the idle treble strings, but not so hard that those strings are held down to the fretboard). Your palm should *not* be touching the back of the neck.

**Photo 6**

## Damping Idle Bass Strings with the Fretting Hand

The tip of the first finger should make contact with the side of the (thicker) string immediately below to dampen it. In Photo 7, the G string is held down by the first finger which touches the adjacent D string.

The extra precaution of stubbing the tip of the first finger up against the adjacent bass string also has the effect of flattening the profile of the first finger so that it lies across any unused treble strings.

**Photo 7**

## Mechanics of Fretting Hand

### Rule of Thumb

It is useful to keep the print part of the thumb placed on the top of the neck whenever possible so that you can maintain a handshape that is a halfway house between two extremes: first, where it must disappear behind the neck when playing wide stretches on the lower strings; and second, where it must squeeze towards the fingers for push-bends and vibrato.

### Playing the Bass Strings (see Photo 8a)

The position of the fretting hand changes as you move from the lower strings across to the treble strings. When playing the bass strings:

- Thumb briefly moves behind the neck

- Forearm drops

- Wrist bends with inside of wrist facing upwards and the back of the wrist facing the floor

- Underside of the fingers rests lightly over the idle treble strings

- Shoulder is relaxed

- Elbow hanging loosely by your side

**Photo 8a (Playing the Lower/Thicker Strings)**

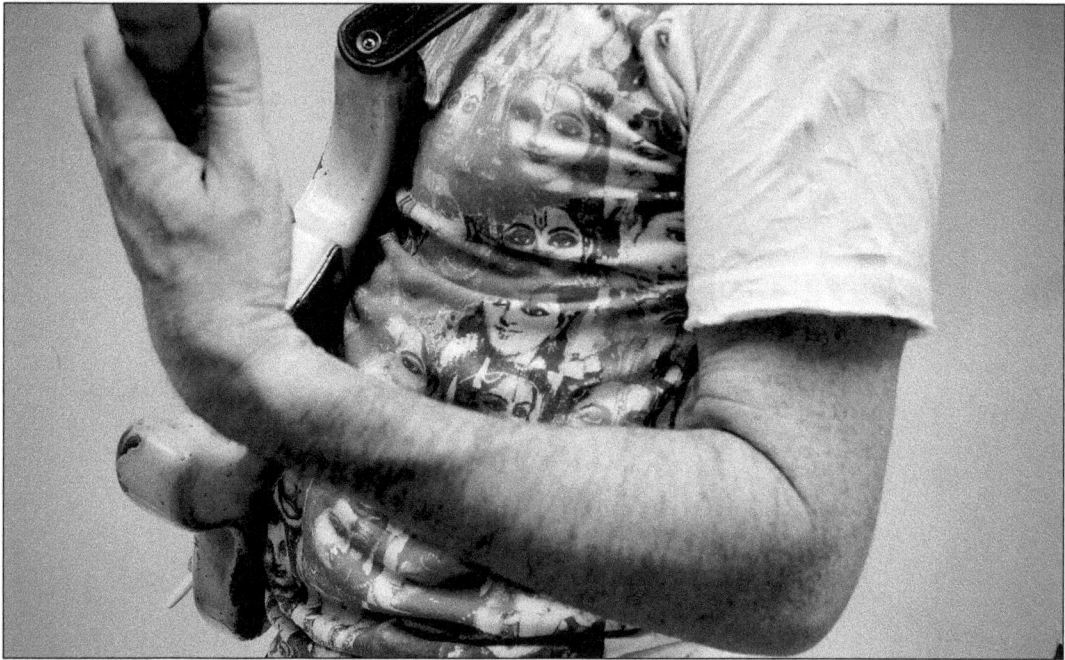

**Playing the Treble Strings (see Photo 8b)**

- Print part of thumb sits on top of the neck

- Forearm raises

- Wrist is straight with inside of wrist facing the guitar body and the back of wrist facing the nut

- The underside of the fingers rest lightly on any unused treble strings

- Shoulder is relaxed

- Elbow hangs loosely by your side

**Photo 8b (Playing the Upper/Thinner Strings)**

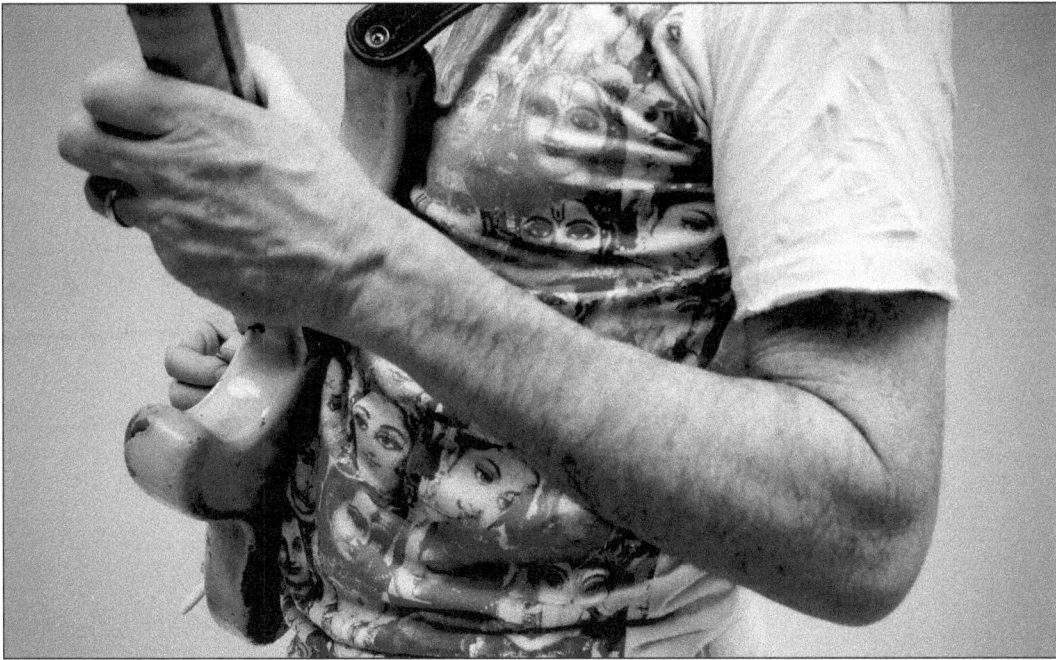

When ascending a scale from the bass to treble strings, remember to keep contact with the inside of the first finger with the underside of the guitar neck as it will act as a natural hinge on which the hand position can turn.

Finally, when moving from a thicker to a thinner string, the final finger to leave the previous string should move directly out from the fretboard (rather than downwards) to ensure that no accidental pull-offs are created.

## Basic Left-Hand Legato Technique

### Quality

To integrate legato musically into your playing, the volume of your hammer-ons and pull-offs should match the volume of your picked notes. To do this, focus on getting as much volume as possible from your fretting hand and lighten your picking, so the picked notes don't overpower the legato ones.

As you work through the following legato exercises, try recording yourself and ask:

- Am I producing a strong, even series of notes?

- Does it sound like a weak mix of faint hammer-ons and pull-offs?

- Is my timing even?

- Are there occasional, overly loud picked notes?

## The Mechanics of a Pull-Off

Many players would find it quite easy to repeat the following notes on the E string without using the pick.

**Example 1a**

[Pick first time only]

After the initial pick, each three-note motif begins with a fourth finger hammer-on, which is relatively easy as it comes down onto the string from height.

However, playing this in the reverse order is a different story because each repeat requires you to use your fourth finger to pull-off from the C to the following A.

**Example 1b**

[Pick first time only]

For players who are new to legato, this pull-off movement is usually so weak that the A is almost inaudible. To fix this, the secret is to pull-off with a downward motion (towards the floor).

Play Example 1b again and try to make the pull-offs between the first and fourth fingers as strong and loud as possible.

To do this:

- Keep the fourth finger relatively straight throughout

- Pull it down towards the floor with a small but powerful turn of the wrist and forearm, rather than using a clawing action with the finger

- With pull-offs in general, keep the tip of the finger in contact with the guitar so that it comes to rest on the adjacent treble string (when present), while remaining over the original fret

Legato normally involves using more muscle groups than just the fingers. For example, if we roll back and forth on the same three notes as shown below, the arm and hand should rock back and forth rather than staying in place and relying on finger-intensive movements.

**Example 1c**

[Pick first time only]

**Timing**

One often overlooked aspect of playing legato is the timing of the fretting hand.

Many players believe that their fretting hand is far more developed than their picking hand, because they can play many notes with their left hand quickly. But when they try to pick the same sequence of notes at the same speed, they struggle. This is usually because the fretting hand isn't moving to a strict and even tempo.

I've often seen students having trouble picking a fast lick or sequence, only to find that it's their fretting hand causing the issue. After practicing the lick using a legato approach, they usually improve at the picked version.

To demonstrate this, start by picking a simple scale passage using 1/16th notes. Play to a metronome, aiming for four notes per click while tapping your foot on each click.

## Example 1d

## Pick Strokes

Where picking is shown in this book (in the initial etudes and short examples), it will be economy picking – the practice of travelling directly to each new string with the pick.

- When travelling from a thick string to a thinner one, use a downstroke

- When travelling from a thin string to a thicker one, use an upstroke

Apart from providing economy of motion, economy picking presents various other advantages which we will discuss a bit further on in this book.

Now try playing the same thing, only picking the first note on each string. You might find that the movement becomes weak, uneven and "triplety" when you are required to hammer-on or pull-off three notes in a row on the same string – especially when playing at speed.

## Example 1e

The key is learning to show restraint and preventing your fretting hand from running ahead of itself. When you pick only the first note on each string, the picked notes often land at odd times within the bar. However, you can't let this disrupt your sense of the 1/16th note division, which can easily happen if the picked notes are much louder than the hammer-ons and pull-offs.

You need to be brutally honest in assessing your timing because any inconsistencies will become obvious when you try to pick the same section. If your hands aren't in sync, it'll show. Record your playing and listen back to it objectively.

## Left-Hand Tapping

*Left-hand tapping* is the term that I use to describe fretting a new string with a hammer-on. (Some players refer to this as a "hammer-on from nowhere").

In the transcriptions this technique is indicated by a square around the hammered note.

As an approach, it has many advantages:

- It helps to declutter passages by stripping out some picked notes. This takes pressure off the picking hand and reduces the amount of picking clicks in fast passages

- It improves the strength and overall quality of the placement of the fretting hand

- By promoting a more positive finger placement it acts as a safety-net even when picking (you'll hear a note even if you miss it with the pick)

- It makes it easier to introduce right-hand taps into your playing, because the right hand is under less time pressure to get back into position to pick subsequent notes

**Using Left-hand Taps When Shifting to a Thicker String.**

Descending a scale typically involves moving to thicker strings, and the first note on each new string being played by the fourth or third finger.

Starting each new string with a left-hand tap is fairly straightforward because the fourth and third fingers can come down from a sufficient height using the first finger as a hinge.

In Example 1f, the first note on each string is played by a high-descending hammer-on using the fourth finger.

**Example 1f**

Ascending a scale normally requires moving to thinner strings, with the first finger playing the first note on each new string. In this case, it's more difficult to start each new string with a left-hand tap as the first finger is typically already clamped down on the fretboard.

**Example 1g**

## Using Left-hand Tapping to Reduce the Amount of Picked Notes

The following exercise shows how a descending three-note scale sequence can be played by only picking the first note on each string.

**Example 1h**

The issue here is that the middle of the figure involves three consecutive picks, which is technically challenging and disrupts the smooth legato effect we're aiming for.

Out of these three picked notes, it's difficult to replace the A with a left-hand tap since it's played with the first finger. However, both of the G notes can be played using a left-hand tap, as the transition is from the high E string to a thicker string, allowing the fourth finger to come down from enough height onto the string.

**Example 1i**

Not only do we reduce the number of picks, but the remaining ones are placed at the start of each beat, making it easier to lock into the rhythm and pulse.

Using economy picking (as shown in both examples) also allows you to follow a helpful rule when picking only the first note on each string: all upstrokes can be replaced with left-hand taps.

Although I will remind you of this rule throughout the legato etudes, it's a good idea to practice each piece both ways (with upstrokes or with left-hand taps). This will give you the flexibility to adapt to various practical situations, such as using different gain settings on your amp or playing with a different string action.

# Chapter Two: Left-hand Legato Etudes to Strict Rhythms

Since timekeeping is crucial when mastering legato, we will begin with two etudes that focus on strict rhythms: the first uses constant 1/16th notes and the second uses 1/8th note triplets.

## "Hard Left"

Although mainly in the key of C, you'll notice a G# note in bars four and twelve where an E7 chord appears in the chord sequence. Normally, the key of C includes an Em chord, but it's common for composers to change this to E or E7 when followed by an Am chord. By changing the G in Em to G#, you add a note that provides a rich tension and creates a strong resolution as it resolves to the A in the Am chord.

## Bars 1–4

This section requires you to play along the length of a single string without picking. The goal is to avoid making the position shifts audible by introducing unwritten slides. The listener should hear a smooth, continuous stream of liquid-sounding 1/16th notes.

There needs to be tight coordination between the first and fourth fingers. Occasionally, you'll need to hammer on a note with your fourth finger while holding down a note a semitone below with your first finger.

For example, when moving from the last note in bar one to the first note in bar two, you must avoid lifting off the E note before hammering onto the F, otherwise there will be a break in the continuity between the two notes.

To develop this close interplay between your first and fourth fingers, I recommend practicing a semitone trill on the high E string using these two fingers. Focus on creating a V-shape with both fingers while maintaining contact between the inside of your first finger and the underside of the neck.

**Photo 9**

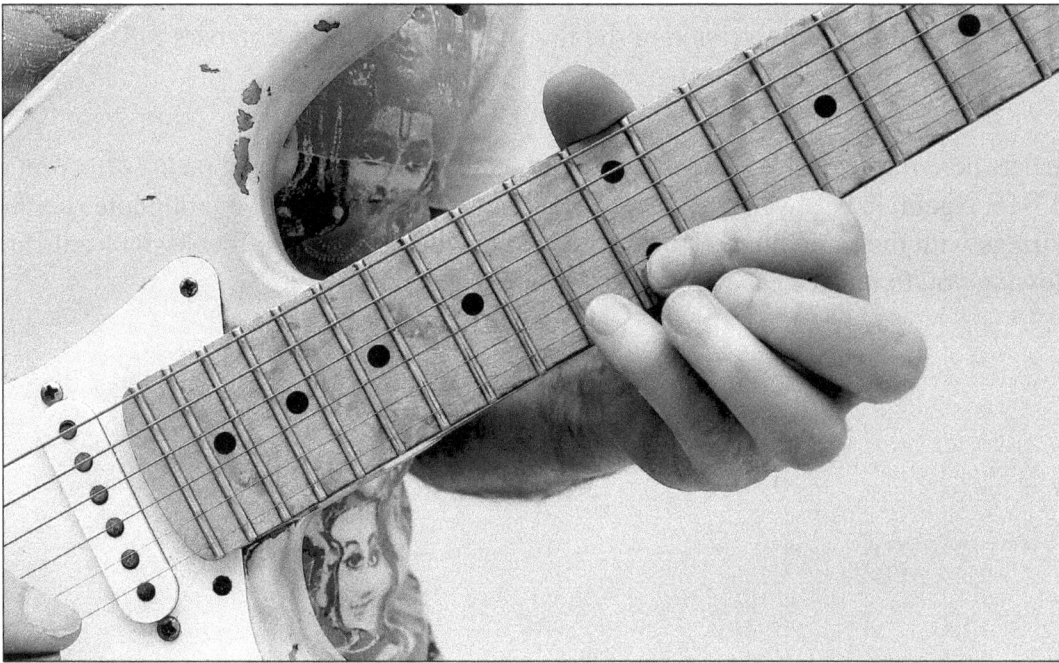

**Bars 5–8**

This section focuses on an ascending four-note scale sequence. Pay attention to the fingering from the middle of bar seven onwards. The idea is to assign a separate finger to each note, allowing you to replace any upstrokes with left-hand taps.

**Bars 9–12**

This section mirrors the first four bars in reverse. It's designed to challenge your ability to make seamless position shifts by compressing and stretching your fretting hand as you perform tone- and semitone-wide pull-offs between the first and fourth fingers. As space tightens near the top of the neck in bars eleven and twelve, notice the suggested switch to your third finger instead of the fourth to maintain fluidity.

**Bars 13–16**

Each bar in this section features a two-note scale sequence as we descend through the scale. In the second half of bar thirteen, the notes across the B and G strings at the 12th and 10th frets could be played using a barré roll. This technique involves redistributing the weight of a single finger across consecutive strings within the same fret. However, I have avoided this and provided a fingering that uses a separate finger for each note. While this may feel awkward or unnatural at first, it allows you to continue transitioning to thicker strings (in this case, the G string) with a hammer-on from the fretting hand, effectively replacing all upstrokes with left-hand taps.

**Bars 17–22**

This passage is designed to test the timekeeping of your fretting hand. Each two-bar section systematically changes the fingering to cover every possible rhythmic permutation. The pick will come in and out at various points, but you must stay focused on playing precise 1/16th notes without letting the picking disrupt your rhythm. This section prioritises practical technique over melodic beauty, so you need to be brutally honest in assessing how well you are staying in time throughout.

**Bars 23–24**

These two bars feature a descending version of the four-note scale sequence in bars 5-8.

**Bars 25–28**

The first three bars here focus on an ascending two-note scale sequence, in the opposite direction to the pattern used in bars 13-16. Again, in bar twenty-eight, you could use a barré roll to play both notes on the 10th fret of the D and A strings with the same finger. However, I've provided a fingering that assigns a different finger to each note, allowing you to replace each upstroke with a left-hand tap.

# Hard Left

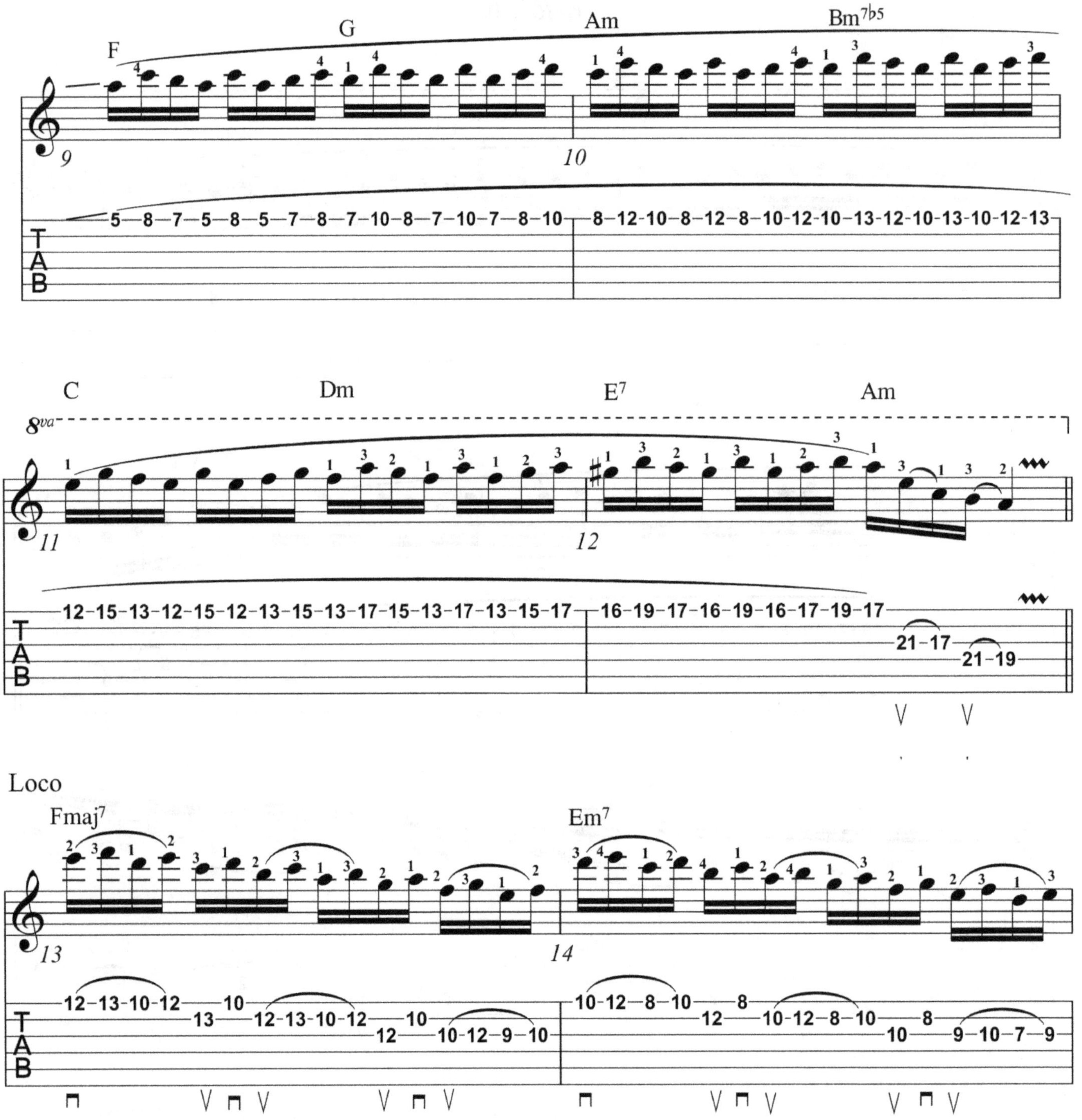
F
G
Am
Bm7b5
C
Dm
E7
Am
8va
Loco
Fmaj7
Em7
TAB

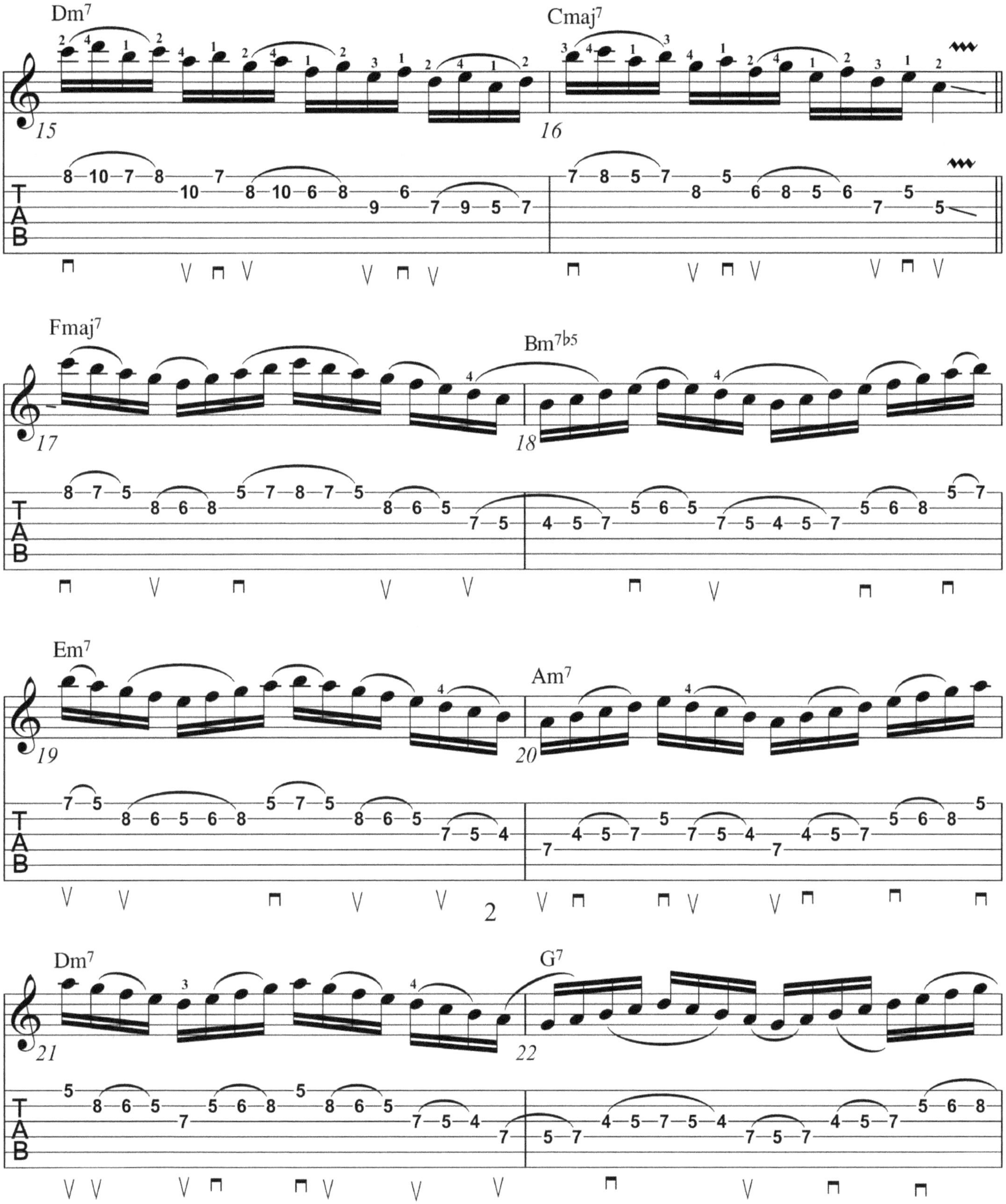
Dm7
Cmaj7
Fmaj7
Bm7♭5
Em7
Am7
Dm7
G7
TAB

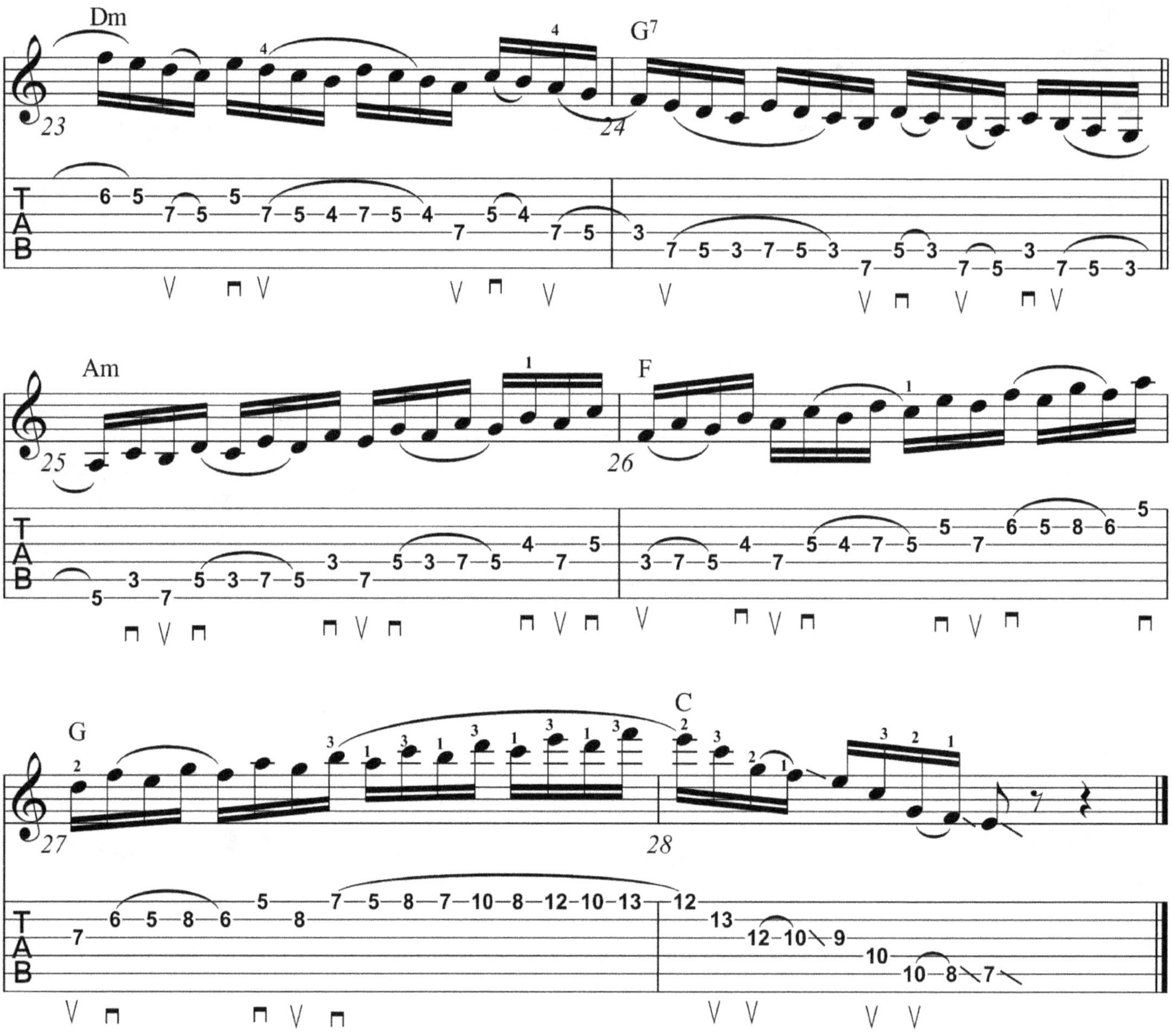
Dm
G7
Am
F
G
C
TAB

## "Trinity"

This technical study piece combines the key skills needed to develop left-hand legato and features constant 1/8th note triplets throughout.

Musically, some sections of Trinity might sound better when played with a mix of legato and picking. But by concentrating on legato here, you'll ensure that when you eventually combine it with other techniques your legato will be as strong and developed as possible.

### Bars 1-3

This opening passage features a straight descent of the scale repeated three times. Because the figure is eleven notes long instead of twelve, it becomes rhythmically displaced when repeated and the whole figure shifts forward by one note each time, causing the notes that fall on the downbeat to change.

- The first note on each string in bar one

- The second note on each string in bar two

- The third (last) note on each string in bar three

Things tend to get tougher as the bars progress because there is a natural tendency for most players to rush a consecutive series of pull-offs on a single string, causing them to arrive at the last one early. Consequently, bar three really tests your powers of restraint to not finish prematurely.

To add to the task, the pick is used on different parts of the beats in each bar.

- The first note of each triplet in bar one

- The third note of each triplet in bar two

- The second note of each triplet in bar three

Rather than trying to play through the entire section, start by breaking things down so that you learn each bar beat-by-beat before trying to piece everything together.

### Bars 4-6

These three bars represent the ascending equivalent of bars 1-3 and will test your timekeeping when applying consecutive hammer-ons on each string.

Once again, the eleven-note figure becomes rhythmically displaced each time it is repeated and things become progressively difficult. By bar six, you will need to show restraint to avoid arriving at the last note of a string of hammer-ons too early.

The following notes must be placed on the downbeat:

- The first note on each string in bar four

- The middle note on each string in bar five

- The third (last) note on each string in bar six

## Bars 7-10

As with bars 1-4 and 9-12 of Hard Left, this section tests your ability to move along the length of a single string without picking. It involves a combination of stretched-out and closed-up finger positioning between the first and fourth fingers of the fretting hand (sometimes spanning five frets, sometimes only one). Make sure there are no audible position shifts with the fretting hand as no slides are used in this section.

## Bars 11-12

In these two bars, you will descend and ascend through the same three-note-per-string scale pattern using three-note melodic figures, starting with the middle finger each time.

## Bars 13-19

This section is the ascending counterpart to bars 7-10. It involves wide and shorter pull-offs between the fourth and first fingers.

## Bar 20

In this section, the first finger (which plays the last note of each pull-off sequence on each string) consistently lands on the downbeat. Similar to bar three, you need to focus on hitting the last note on each string at the correct time during this descending pull-off scale run.

Additionally, after the initial note, the pick is used on the middle note of each triplet. It's crucial not to accidentally place these picked notes on the downbeat as you increase the tempo. If you're struggling with this, slow everything down, play to a metronome, and ensure you can play and count the rhythm accurately before speeding up.

The same principle is also used in the final two bars.

## Bars 21-22

This is a straightforward ascending/descending three-note scale sequence using the C Major Pentatonic scale, which has the same notes as A Minor Pentatonic (A, C, D, E, G).

## Bars 23-24

These bars feature a three-note pentatonic scale sequence, this time using Bm7b5 Pentatonic scale which also exists in the key of C Major.

| Bm7b5 Pentatonic Scale | B | D | E | F | A |
|---|---|---|---|---|---|
| Formula | 1 | b3 | 4 | b5 | b7 |

## Bars 25-30

In this section, we alternate between descending and ascending three-note scale sequences in the key of C on the B and E strings.

These kinds of three-note scale sequences are excellent for building and maintaining stamina in your fretting hand.

Slides are included to improve your ability to make lateral shifts without losing momentum. Make sure everything stays in strict 1/8th note triplets throughout.

## Getting the Most Out of Each Piece

It's possible to get a lot of mileage from both Hard Left and Trinity. You can:

- Play each study as written

- Eliminate all the upstrokes and replace them with left-hand taps

- Use them as a picking workout (picking every note). This is actually a good idea when working through each study for the first time, as it allows you to focus on learning the notes without being distracted by the legato technique

- Additionally, you can challenge your picking hand even more by palm muting everything throughout

# Trinity

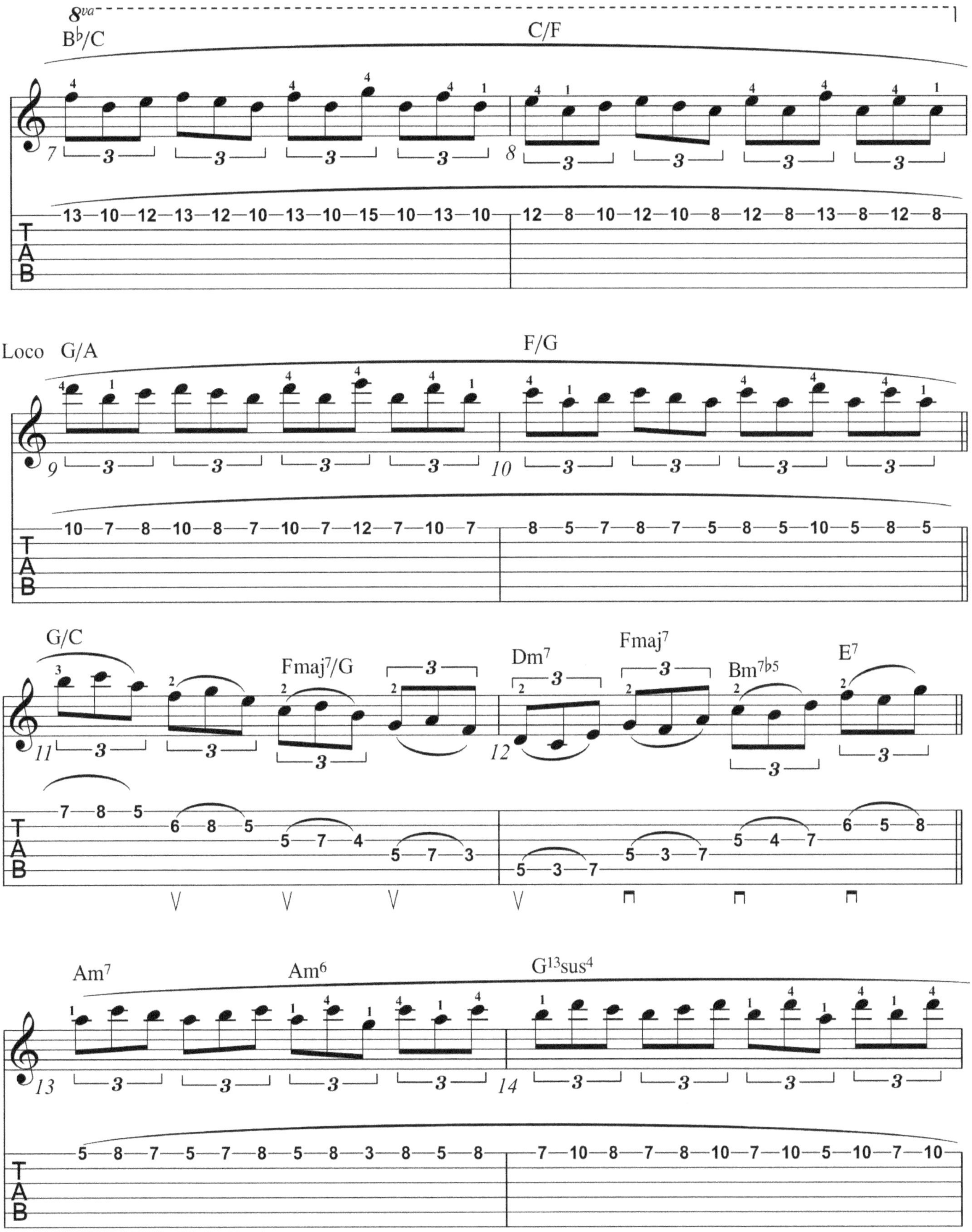
8va
B♭/C
C/F
Loco
G/A
F/G
G/C
Fmaj7/G
Dm7
Fmaj7
Bm7♭5
E7
Am7
Am6
G13sus4

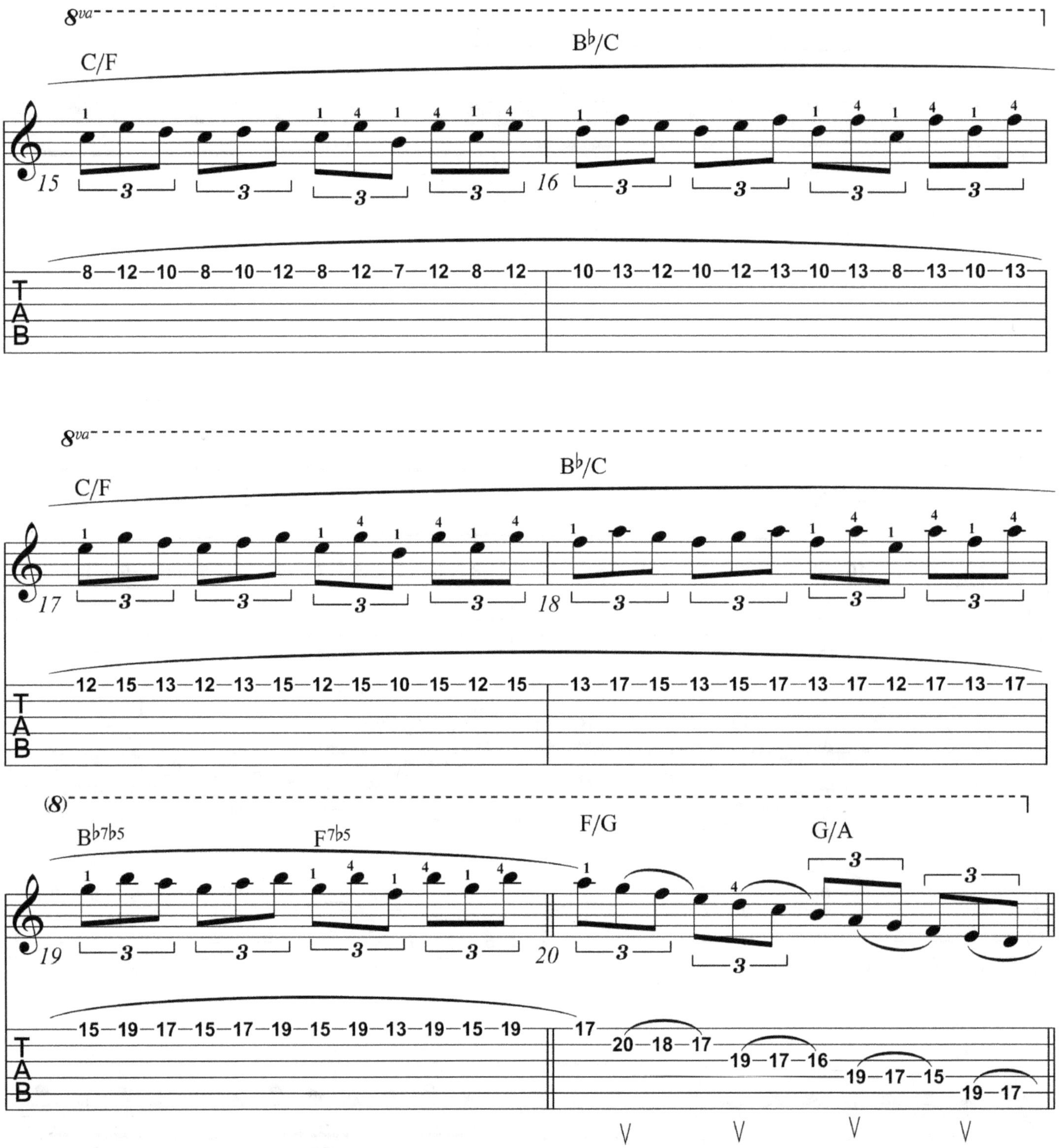
8va
C/F
B♭/C
8va
C/F
B♭/C
(8)
B♭7♭5
F7♭5
F/G
G/A
TAB

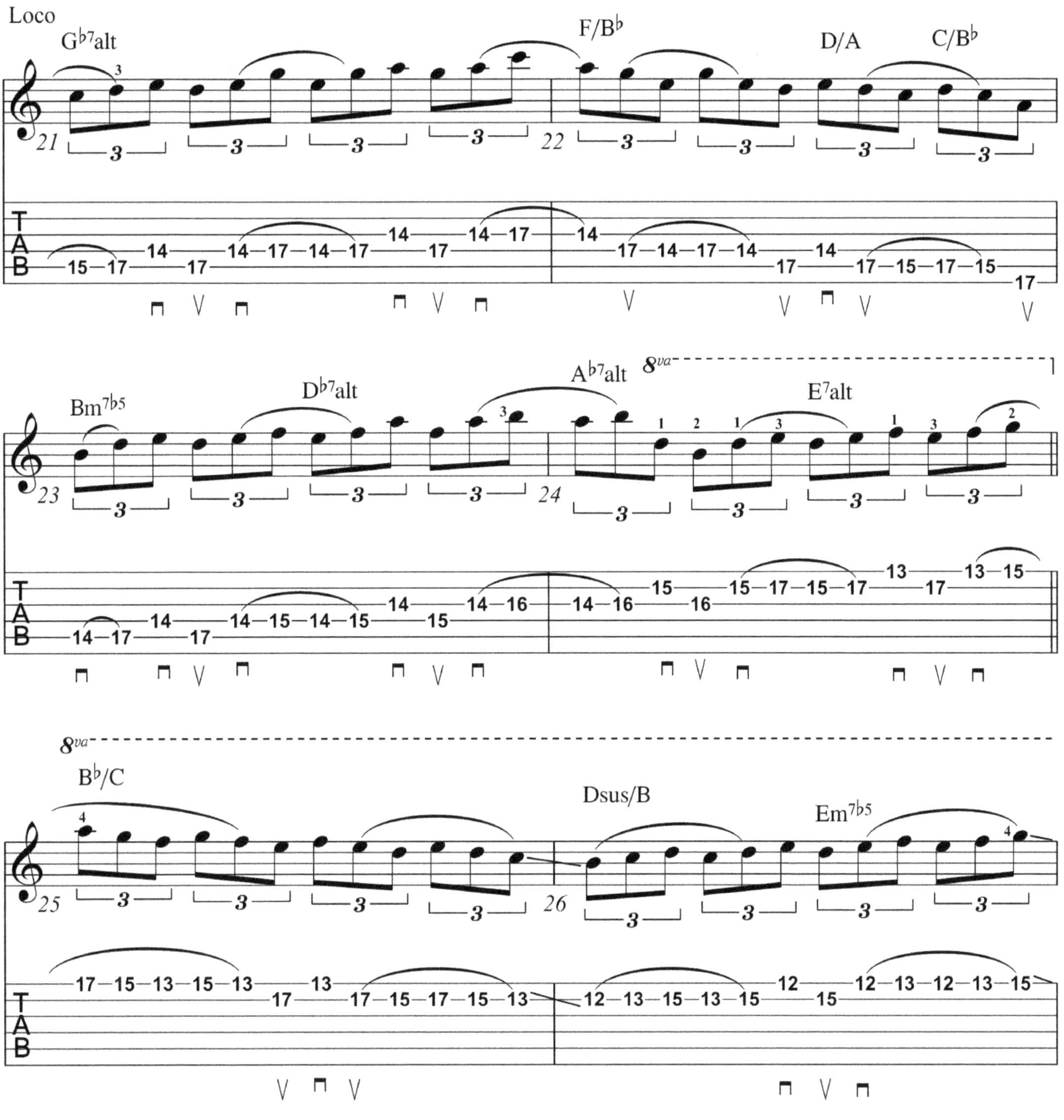
Loco
G♭7alt
F/B♭
D/A
C/B♭
Bm7♭5
D♭7alt
A♭7alt
8va
E7alt
8va
B♭/C
Dsus/B
Em7♭5

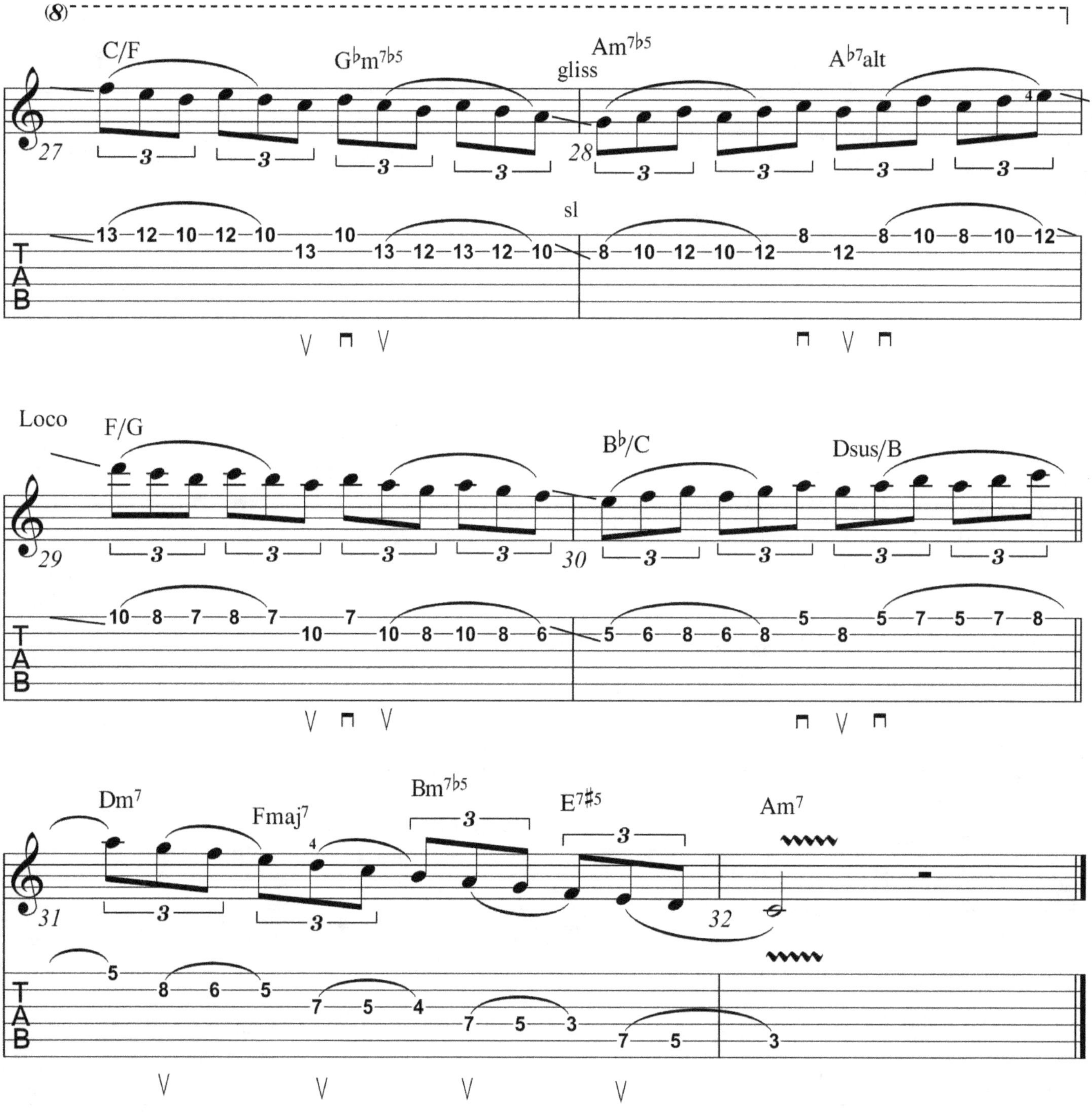
(8)
C/F
G♭m7♭5
gliss
Am7♭5
A♭7alt
sl
Loco
F/G
B♭/C
Dsus/B
Dm7
Fmaj7
Bm7♭5
E7♯5
Am7

# Chapter Three: Playing Odd Note Groupings

So far, we've focused on legato examples played evenly to build your timing, as rhythmic control is essential for left-hand legato. However, the mechanics of legato often lead to odd-note rhythmic groupings which can sound more organic and less regimented than traditional four- or six-note groupings.

Example 3a demonstrates how five-note groupings are naturally formed while rolling forwards and backwards using three-notes-per-string. Let's begin with quintuplets which are five notes squeezed into the space of each beat.

**Example 3a**

With this repeated circular figure, if you focus on placing the picked notes on the click and evenly distributing the notes in between, the rhythms should naturally fall into place.

Similarly, if you roll forwards, backwards, and then forwards on each string while playing three-notes-per-string, you'll end up with a seven-note grouping (septuplets). Again, focus on targeting the picked notes on the beat and try to spread the other notes as evenly as possible.

**Example 3b**

## Destination Points

Due to this natural tendency towards odd note-groupings, legato often floats over the music to create a fluid stream of notes. So, rather than focusing on the exact rhythms of the note divisions, you can simply concentrate on targeting specific destination notes.

At high speeds, timekeeping is less critical. In fact, beyond a certain speed, as long as the notes are spaced evenly, you can speed up or slow down a repeated figure and the listener will accept it. However, if the notes are spaced unevenly, the result will sound "lumpy".

With practice, you'll be able to naturally stretch or compress a series of notes to fit evenly into the allotted space.

This approach is often a revelation to amateur guitar players because they're often used to reading transcriptions of fast guitar solos that are filled with rhythmic complexities (odd note-groupings, nested tuplets, etc.)

By meticulously transcribing exactly what was played, the transcriber can sometimes lose the original intent of the player, and the chaotic rhythms presented on the page don't accurately reflect what the guitarist had in mind. Those daunting rhythms are often just a byproduct of the player slightly accelerating and decelerating throughout a phrase when targeting a particular destination note.

# Chapter Four: Left-hand Legato Etudes Featuring Mixed Rhythms

## "Continuum"

This etude features a wide variety of approaches: palm-muted left-hand tapping, septuplet rolls, lateral motion, circular patterns, 1/32nd notes, barré rolls, nine-note groupings, nested quintuplets, 1/16th note triplets and string skipping.

### Bars 1-2

This first section is reminiscent of Greg Howe, who often combines palm muting with left-hand tapping to create a percussive effect.

### Bars 3-4

Like Example 3b, this example also uses septuplets, but instead of simply rolling forwards and backwards on the three notes of each string, we're introducing a new pattern. It might feel strange at first, but with enough practice, it will become natural. Eventually, once you pick the first note (fretted using the first finger), the rest of the pattern should flow automatically.

As before, the key is to focus on placing the picked notes on the click and evenly distributing the notes in between. If done correctly, the rhythm should take care of itself.

### Bar 5

This bar features a neo-classic-style pedal-point melody that sounds really sweet using a legato approach.

### Bars 7-8

This ascending legato pattern spans three strings and is reminiscent of one used by Uli Jon Roth in the Scorpions' track *Sails of Charon*. While his pattern descends in B Harmonic Minor, here we ascend C Major.

### Bars 9-10

If you want to use legato to move freely around the fretboard, it's good to practice licks that move in circles.

The repeated thirty-two-note lick in these two bars is split into two halves. The first half moves anticlockwise and the second half moves clockwise.

Don't worry about counting the 1/32nd notes, instead practice this lick by focusing on inching your way from one target note to the next, and aim to fit all the other notes in between. If you maintain an even spacing between the notes, the rhythm will naturally fall into place. It may take some time to build up to the fast demo speed, so focus on mastering it slowly first.

### Bars 11-12

The rhythms in this section are much easier to play than they may look. Just listen to the track and follow the keyboard line. Again, you'll probably have to spend time learning this at a slower speed.

### Bar 13

This bar introduces a concept known as *nested tuplets*, where fast groups of notes are placed within an underlying rhythmic structure. In this case, we have quintuplets nested inside a 1/4 note triplet pulse.

In Example 3a, we created quintuplets by placing the first note of each five-note group on the downbeat. Here, you need to place those first notes on the 1/4 note triplet pulse instead. If you do that and distribute the other notes evenly, everything should fall into place.

**Bar 14**

Here we see a triplet version of the two-note descending scale sequence used in Hard Left, specifically in bars 13-16. Note how the same "2 against 3" rhythmic principle is also applied in bar twenty.

Again, don't be thrown off by the pick coming in at awkward rhythmic points.

Just as the upstrokes in previous examples can be replaced with left-hand taps, here the left-hand taps can be replaced with upstrokes.

**Bars 15-16**

We have more 1/16th note triplets in these bars, but they also feature an ascending pattern that is nine notes long (indicated in brackets). Some of these nine-note patterns include a 4th interval which requires the use of a barré roll. For this, lay the finger flat to play consecutive notes on different strings within the same fret, and redistribute the finger's pressure using your wrist and arm, rather than changing the shape of the finger.

Don't worry if you don't get much separation between the notes when using a barré roll. A 4th interval is consonant and has a rock 'n' roll feel, so it won't sound bad if the notes blend into each other a bit.

**Bars 17-18**

As in bar thirteen, these two bars feature more 1/16th note groupings (both four and five) played against a 1/4 note triplet pulse. The 1/4 note triplet pulse is especially easy to hear in this section as it's outlined by each note on the high E string.

While I used economy picking in the recording – downstrokes on the high E string and upstrokes on the G string – you may choose to pick it differently. For example, you could use hybrid picking, where the middle finger of your picking hand plucks upwards on the E string while the pick applies downstrokes to the G string.

**Bar 19**

Some more barré rolls appear here. To play the septuplets, focus on targeting the first note of each seven-note pattern (on the high E string) to align with the downbeat. If you keep the spacing between the other notes even, the septuplet rhythms will fall into place automatically.

# Continuum

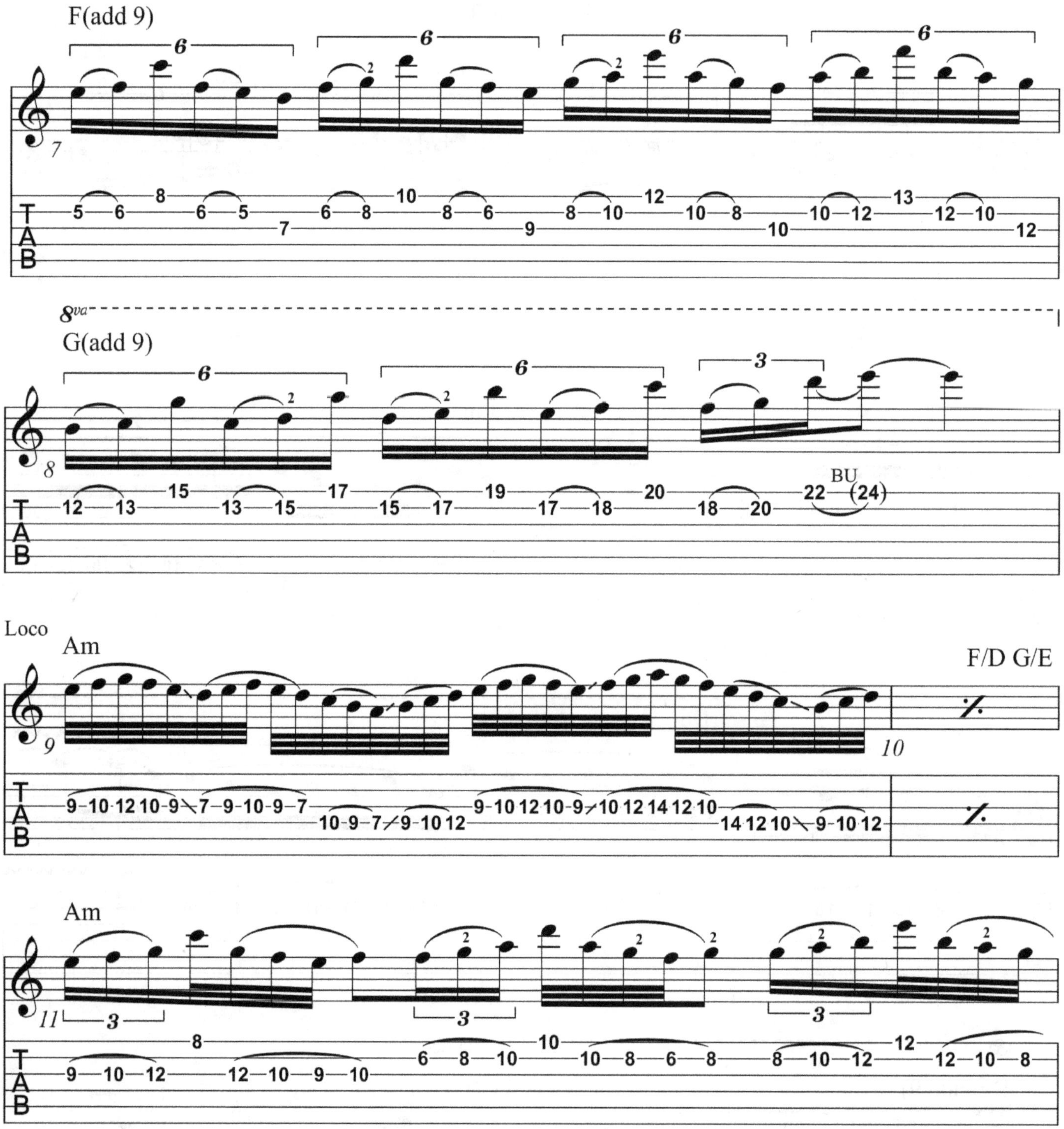
F(add 9)
8va
G(add 9)
BU
Loco
Am
F/D G/E
Am

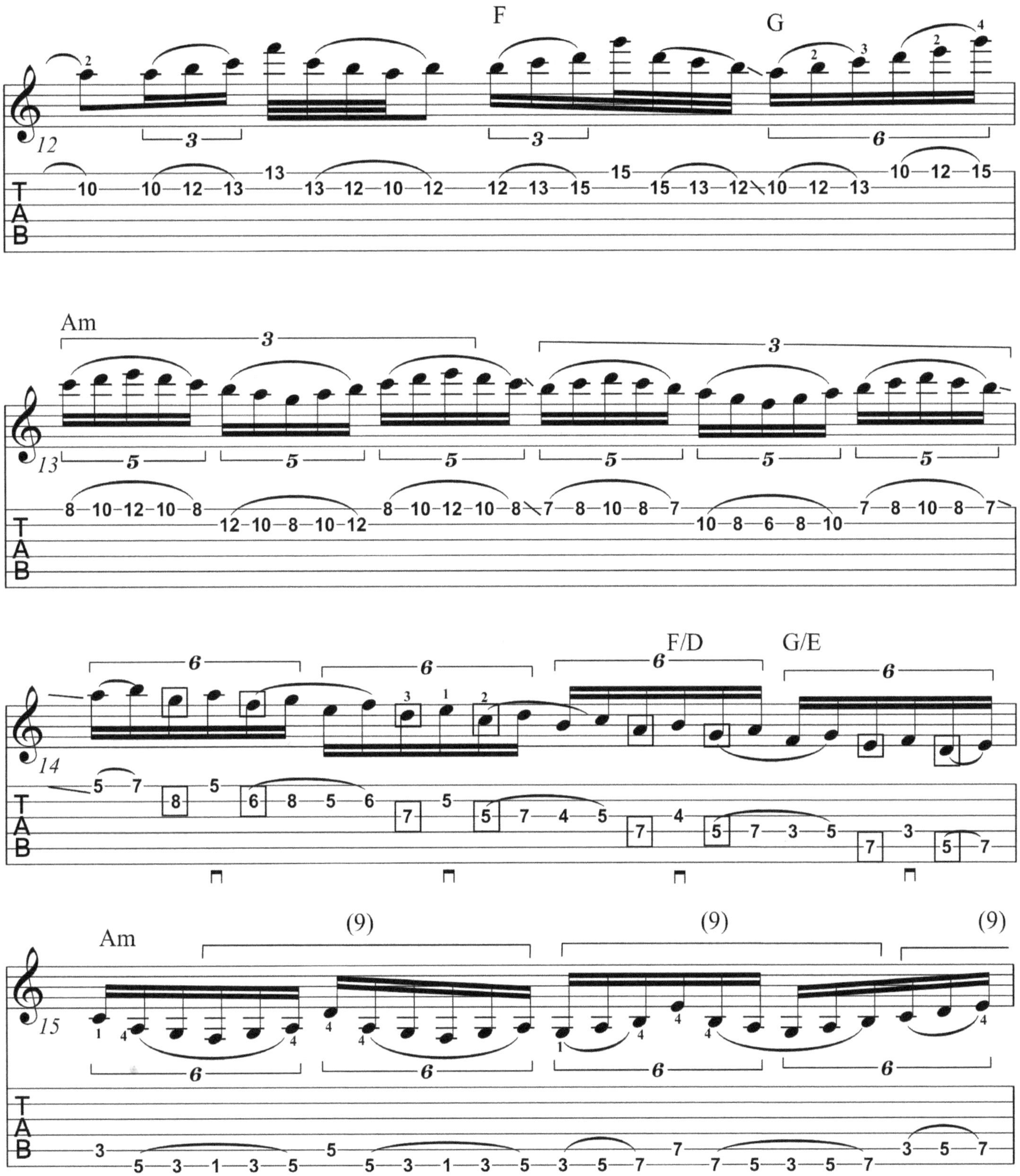
F
G
Am
F/D
G/E
Am
(9)
(9)
(9)

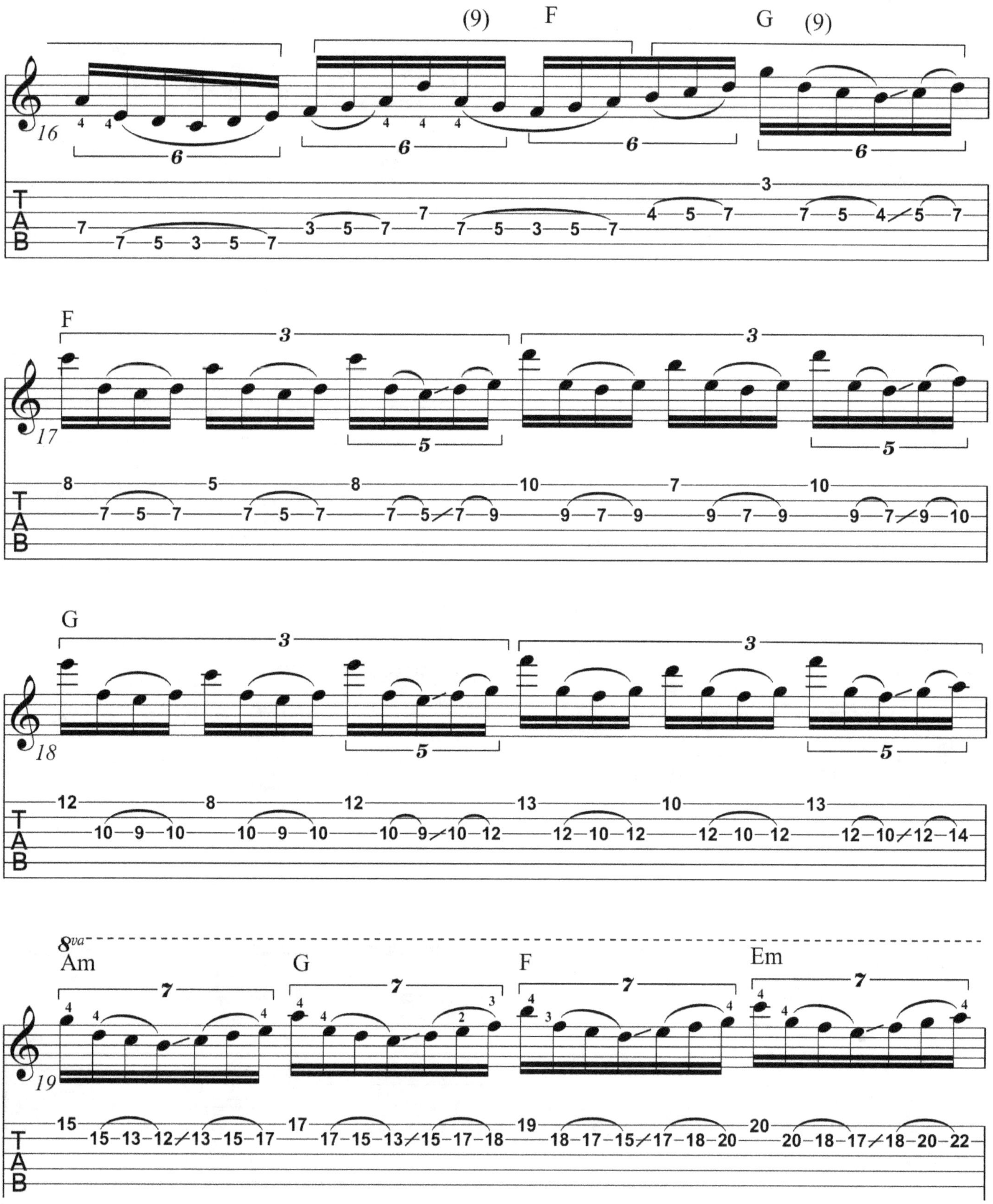
(9)
F
G
(9)
F
G
8va
Am
G
F
Em
TAB

(8)-------------------------------------------------------------------¬

G(6)/D        Am(add b6)/E    Bo(add b6)/F    C(maj7)/G        Am

```
T  |--22--19---------20--17-----------------19--15-----------------------|
A  |---------20--17----------18--15-------------------17----------------|
B  |--------------------------------------------------------16----17~----|
   20                                                 21
```

## "Unbroken Chain"

This etude explores a variety of technical approaches such as wide stretches, 4ths, and consecutive quintuplets. Note that there are many diatonic patterns, where a motif is followed by a series of similar shapes taken further up the scale, adjusting the notes each time to stay within the key (for example in bars 3-4, 5-6, 7-8).

### Bars 1-2

The solo starts with an ascending four-note scale sequence followed by a descending two-note scale sequence. The left-hand taps in bar two are optional; these notes can be picked instead. However, mastering this technique will make playing sequences like this at speed much easier.

### Bars 3-4

Bar three begins with an ascending eight-note sequence which is then shifted up the neck, with each note moving one scale note higher each time.

### Bars 5-6

Each of these bars contains a classical-style pedal point pattern with wide stretches. The fingering can be tricky, so follow the transcription, which suggests using just the first, second, and fourth fingers.

### Bars 7-8

This section features ascending quintuplets, each with an added slide. As with Example 3a, focus on the destination points. Each note on the high E string is played on the downbeat, and aim for even spacing between the other notes to help the quintuplets fall naturally into place.

### Bars 9-12

This section consists entirely of perfect 4th intervals played on a single string. Wide stretches like this emphasise that much of legato is not just finger-intensive but is often accompanied by a slightly lower arm action, creating a small wrist rotation that helps lift the fourth finger on and off the fretboard. Be careful with these stretches if you're not used to them. Take it easy and don't overdo it at first. Large stretches are very demanding until your hand has been conditioned through short and regular progressive practice.

**Bars 13-16**

This is the first of two sections that combine quintuplets and sextuplets. You'll need to analyse the twenty-three notes in each bar and identify the four that need to land on the click. Start with a slow metronome and gradually increase the tempo as you improve. At first, you might want to hold each target note (the ones that land on the click) a bit longer to clearly hear where they should fall. Then, as you increase the metronome speed, work on evening out the spaces between all the notes.

**Bars 17-22**

This section mixes quintuplets and sextuplets and is also in a different time signature (3/4 instead of 4/4). Again, focus on the notes that fall on the click and, if necessary, follow the process mentioned earlier. Note that the fourth finger occasionally barrés to play adjacent notes on the G and E strings.

Bar 22 introduces three different note groupings on each beat: 5, 6, and 4 notes. Additionally, it features a G# note that doesn't belong to the key of C but reflects the G# Diminished chord in the underlying progression.

**Bars 23-24**

Here, the time signature changes to 2/4. In the second half of bar 24, another G# note appears, reflecting the major third of the accompanying E chord (E, G#, B).

**Bars 25-26**

The study finishes with an A Minor arpeggio, played using legato and wide stretches. Use the first and fourth fingers of your fretting hand throughout.

We return to 4/4 time here, but don't be intimidated by the time signature changes. Listen to the music until you can sing the part, then play what you hear in your head rather than focusing on what you see on the page.

# Unbroken Chain

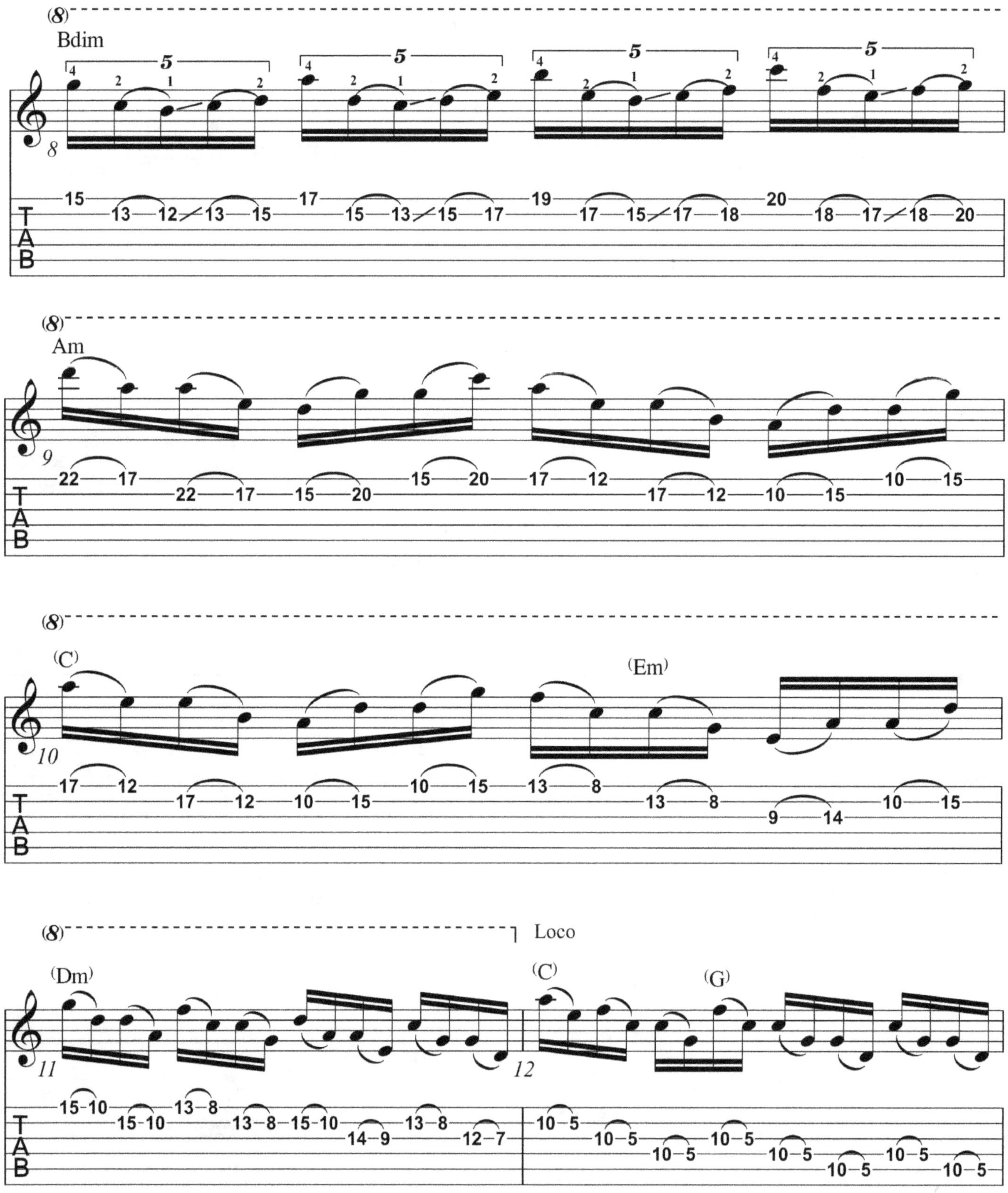
(8)
Bdim
(8)
Am
(8)
(C)
(Em)
(8)
Loco
(Dm)
(C)
(G)

F/A

G/E

F/D

G

51

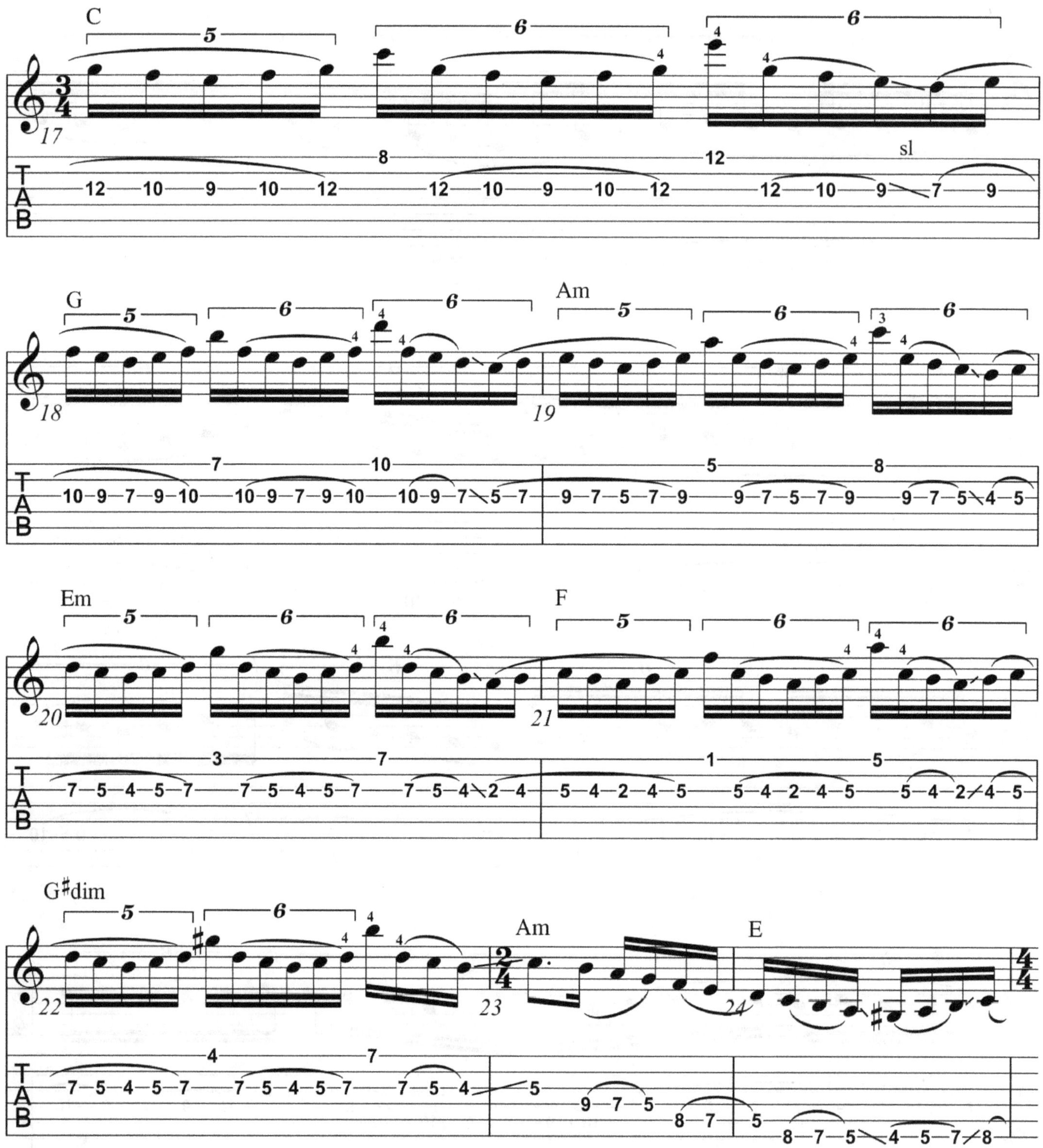
C
sl
G
Am
Em
F
G♯dim
Am
E

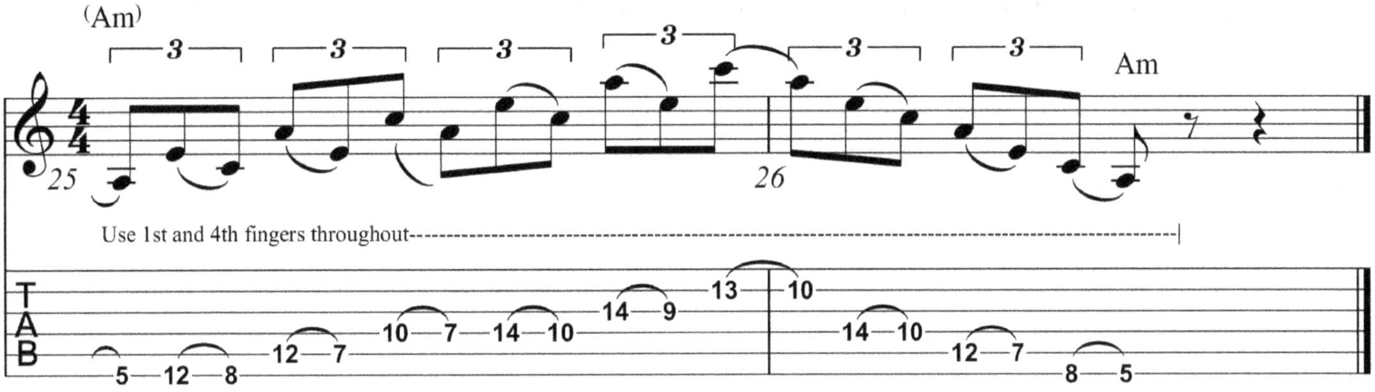
(Am)
Am
Use 1st and 4th fingers throughout
TAB

# Chapter Five: Combining Right- and Left-hand Tapping

Right-Hand Tapping is the practice of adding hammer-ons and pull-offs using one or more fingers of the picking hand. It's usually used in conjunction with left-hand legato and indicated in the transcriptions with a circle around each note.

**Tap with the Second Finger**

Modern rock players frequently blend picking and tapping in their solos, so it's essential to keep holding the pick between your thumb and first finger while tapping. The second finger is ideal for tapping since it's the longest and centrally positioned, making it convenient for the technique.

Other Considerations (see Photos 10a and 10b):

- Ensure that you rest the side of your right hand (karate chop-style) on all the idle bass strings

- Try tilting the tapping hand so that the palm is turned towards your face. This ensures you make contact on the string with the inside edge of the tapping finger

- I recommend that you tap *upwards* with the tapping finger. Tapping towards the floor is mechanically inefficient and tends to involve a hand motion (rather than just the finger), which makes it difficult to reduce unwanted noise

Placing the tips of the 3rd and 4th fingers of the right hand on the underside of the neck has several advantages:

- They will serve to act as a physical reference

- They help you to anchor the hand into a stable position

- They can be used to damp any idle treble strings to cut out open string noise

By applying each of the above, you create a channel within which the tapped string can sound while the adjacent strings are damped.

**Photo 10a: Tapping on the Upper/Thinner Strings**

**Photo 10b: Tapping on the Lower/Thicker Strings**

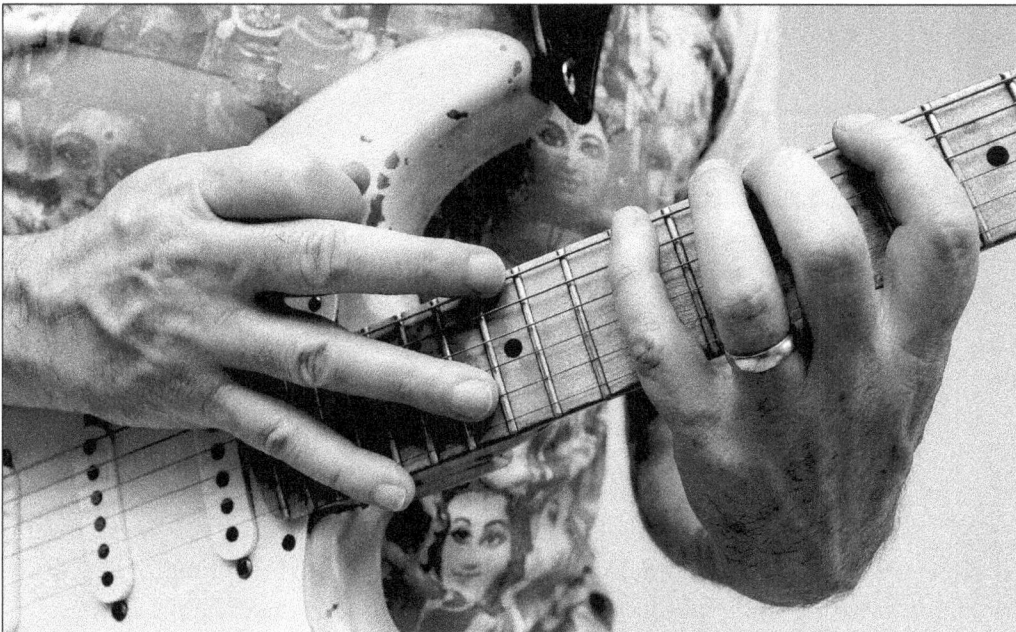

## Tapping On One String

This C Major exercise allows you to focus on the quality of your right-hand tapped notes as the hand remains stationary while you shift the left hand up and down the string.

You can also focus on the quality of the pull-off from each right-hand tap by placing each left hand note on the downbeats. Each note in the left-hand melody should sound clear and strong.

**Example 5a**

## Using Right-hand Taps to Shift from String to String

In the following exercise, the right-hand tap is used to change from string to string. Again, it is essential that you get a strong pull-off from each right-hand tap.

**Example 5b**

One of the most effective things you can practice for tapping is to take a left-hand legato idea and use a right-hand tap to start each new string at the points when you would normally use the pick.

The following example is written as 1/16th note triplets and is similar to Example 3a, played by replacing the picked notes with taps.

**Example 5c**

With a bit of practice, you will be able to adapt all your left-hand legato figures in this way.

### How Left-Hand Taps Help Us to Integrate Right-Hand Taps

The example below shows how left-hand tapping can reduce pressure on the picking hand when adding right-hand taps. By using a left-hand tap for the first note on the B string, the picking hand has time to reposition after tapping, and pick the A note on the E string.

Since you are both picking and tapping with the picking hand, ensure you pick each string near the tapping area (on the neck) instead of moving back and forth between the neck and pickup area.

Combining these various techniques (right-hand tapping, left-hand legato, left-hand tapping, and picking) makes this passage smoother and, once mastered, easier to play than if fully picked.

**Example 5d**

## How Right-hand Taps Allow Us to Use First Finger Left-hand Taps

Right-hand taps make it easier to shift from a thicker string to a thinner one, using a left-hand tap with the first finger. When a right-hand tap is held down, the left hand is freed up, allowing it to lift off the fretboard. This gives the first finger enough height to come down onto the new string with enough force to create a strong note.

**Example 5e**

Technically, you'll need to follow a certain sequence of events to play something like this cleanly:

When playing the first right-hand tap, the left hand must spring up simultaneously, so it's poised to hammer downwards from a height onto the next string.

When the left-hand tap on the high E string is played, simply soften the contact with the tapping finger of the right hand, rather than lift it away completely. This will take the energy out of the string. Leave it gently with the right-hand finger while simultaneously damping that string using the side of the picking hand.

## Assessing Your Fretting Hand Technique

The following exercise teaches you to isolate the placement of your first first finger. It is deceptively difficult and quite revealing, as it places your left-hand technique under a particularly harsh microscope.

When playing this exercise using distortion, most players experience a lot of open-string noise and one of the most difficult parts is getting sufficient strength from the first finger hammer-on.

**Example 5f**

To play this cleanly:

- Damp the E, A, D and G strings with the side of the picking hand. This will leave the B and E as the only strings that can ring

- Place the fingerprint part of the first finger down on the E string so that the tip stubs up against the B string

- Damp the E string with the underside of the second finger as it hammers onto the 6th fret and ensure it stubs up against the G string

Listen out for unwanted string noise and adjust as necessary.

Occasionally, further unwanted noise may also be created by:

- Overshooting instead of accurately stubbing the tip of the first finger up against the B string

- Also holding down the 6th fret of the E string with the first finger when hammering onto the second note in the sequence

You'll find the whole thing difficult at first, but things will start to take shape if you do a little each day.

# Chapter Six: Right- and Left-hand Tapping Featuring Strict Rhythms

The following two etudes focus on strict timekeeping: the first one uses constant 1/8th note triplets, the second one uses constant 1/16th notes.

Up until this point, we have always used the pick when moving to a thinner string. In these two pieces, we will be using either a right- or left-hand tap to start a new string instead.

## "No Picking Allowed-1"

To play in strict time throughout the piece, you will have to demonstrate robotic restraint. This is not the time to be expressive. Be mechanical!

### Bars 1-4

The first part of the tune features a relentless series of triplets, each starting with a left-hand tap using the first finger. This is made possible because the last note on each string is played with a right-hand tap that allows the fretting hand to leave the fretboard and bring the first finger down onto the new string from enough height to produce a strong note.

Refer back to Example 5e to review the precise technique for using right-hand taps in conjunction with the left-hand taps to achieve bold, clear notes without unwanted noise.

For the first eight bars of this piece, use only the first and second fingers of your fretting hand, except where otherwise indicated at the start of bars two and six.

### Bars 5-8

Here, we see triplet sequences played on a series of triad arpeggios. Picking this sequence at speed would be very difficult, yet this tapped version makes it relatively easy to play a lot of notes without having to move your hands and fingers that quickly.

Another factor that makes this method so effective is that the right-hand taps always occur on the first note of each triplet, making it easier to lock into the beat at high tempos.

When playing through this passage, aim for a high and purposeful lifting action with the first finger as it will help strengthen your left-hand tapped notes.

### Bars 9-12

This passage is designed to test the accuracy you built in Example 5f and can result in a lot of unwanted string noise if you aren't accurate. If you're struggling, return to Example 5f and spend more time there.

# No Picking Allowed-1

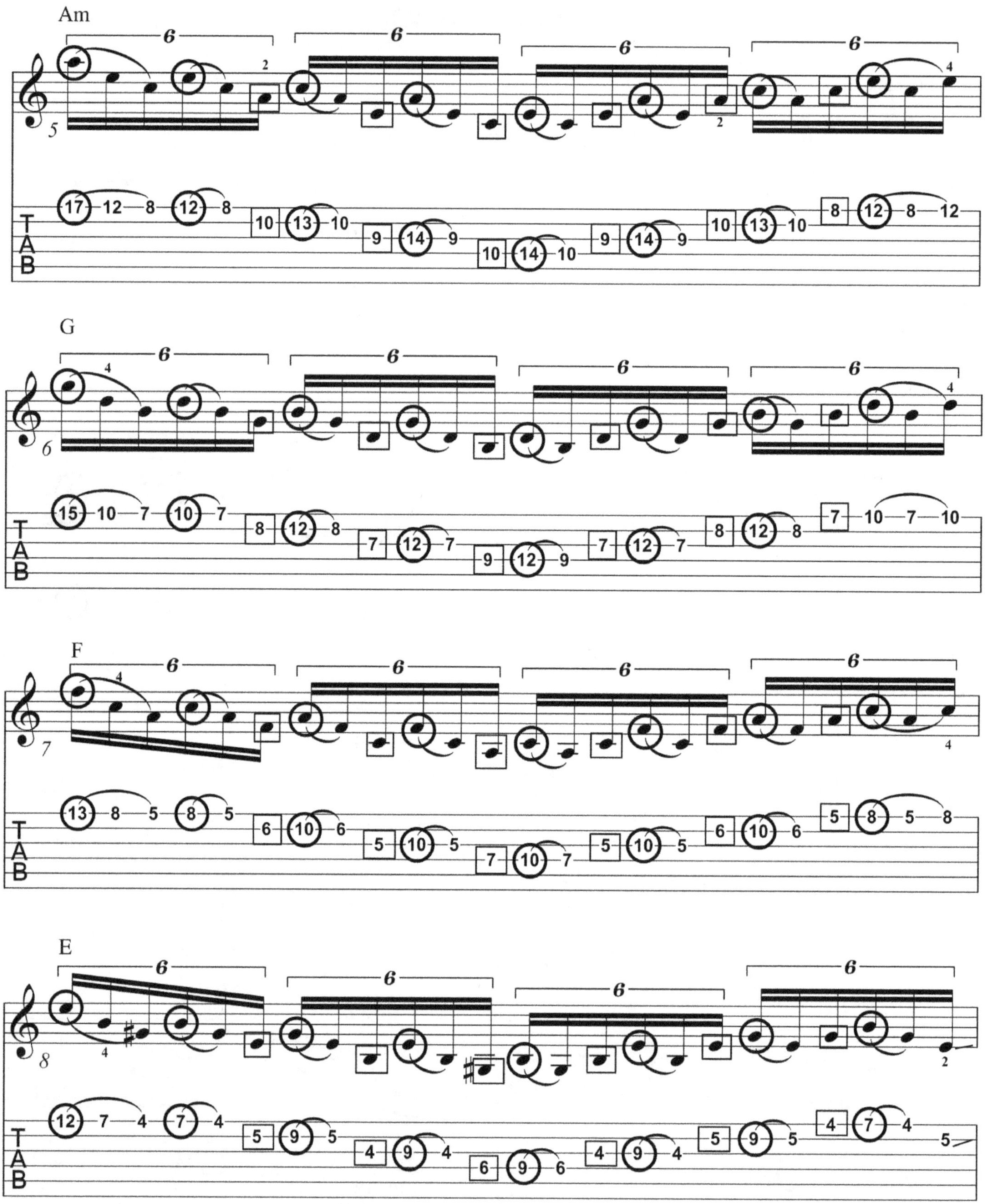
Am
G
F
E

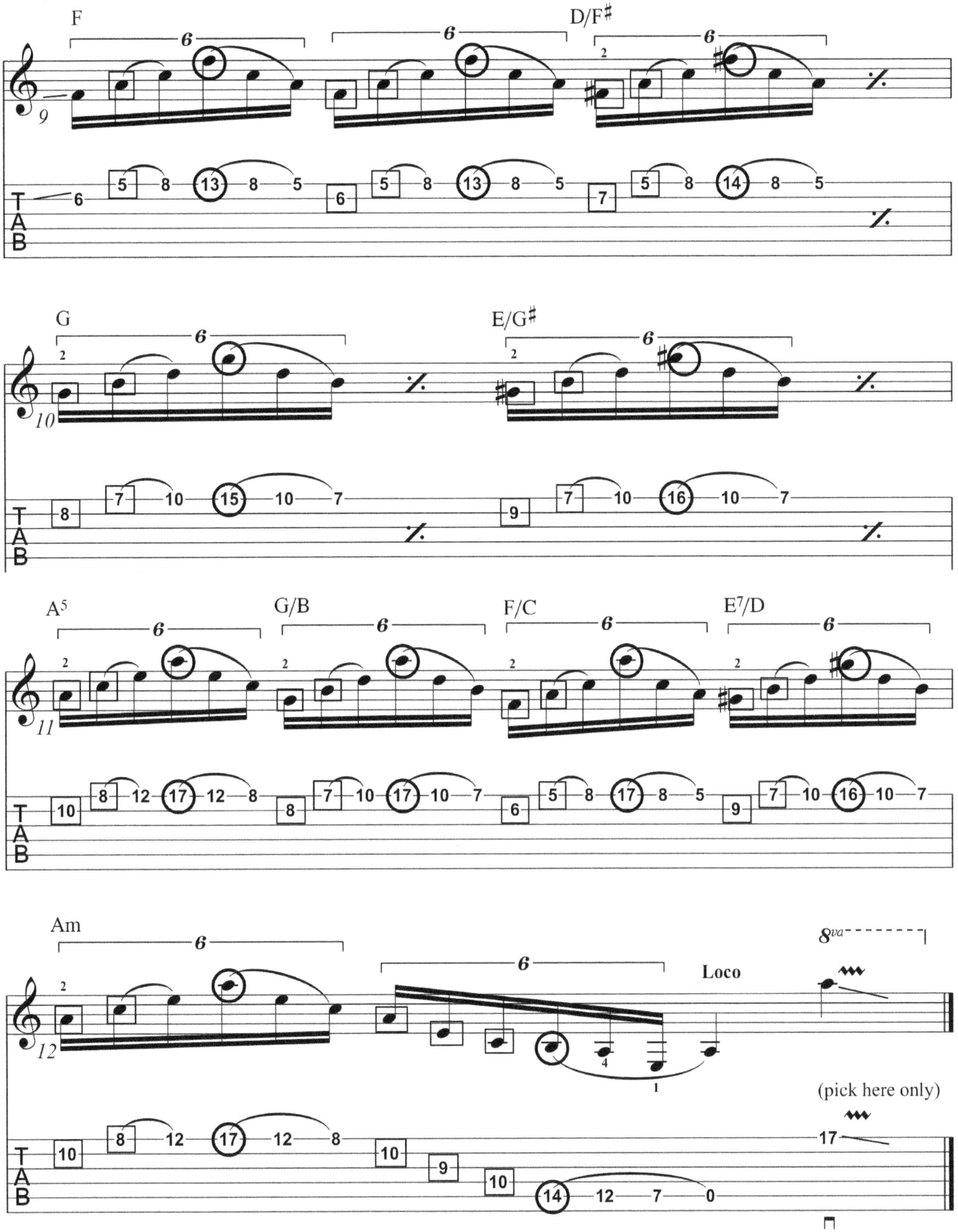
F
D/F♯
G
E/G♯
A5
G/B
F/C
E7/D
Am
Loco
8va
(pick here only)

## "No Picking Allowed-2"

This etude features constant 1/16th notes and integrates all the key skills needed to combine left- and right-hand tapping effectively.

### String Skipping

String-skipping adds an arpeggio-like quality to traditional scale sequences by introducing leaps instead of stepwise movement.

In addition to creating wide intervals, string-skipping can introduce a sense of call and response, or counterpoint, as you shift between notes on different strings. Many players, such as Paul Gilbert, find it easier to play intricate arpeggio passages using string-skipping rather than fingerings suited to sweep picking.

The following two diagrams show how notes of the same arpeggio can be arranged to suit sweep picking or string skipping.

**C Major Arpeggio (Sweep Picking Shape)**

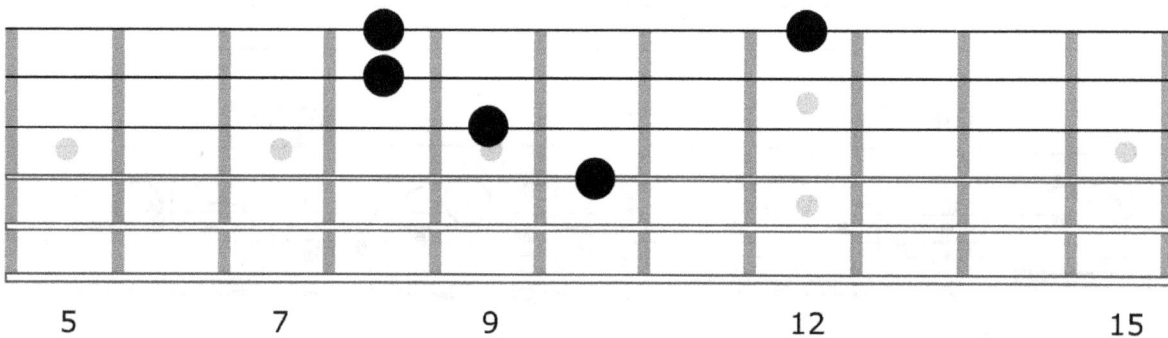

**C Major Arpeggio (Modified Fingering Suitable for String-skipping)**

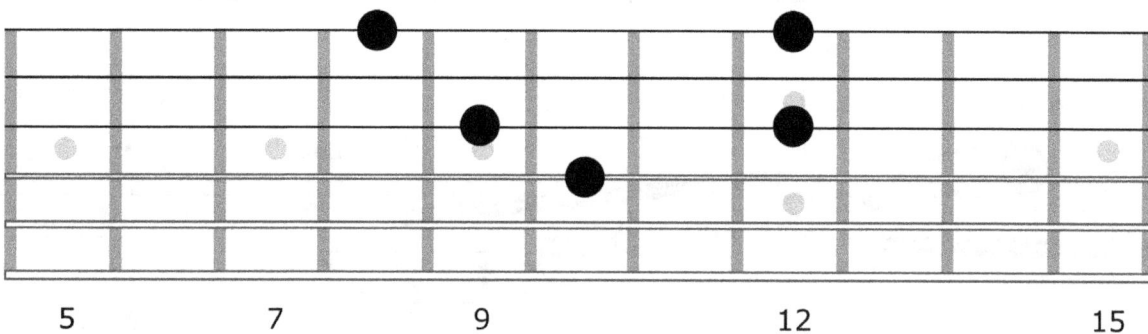

It is also common to combine string skipping with left- and right-hand tapping to play arpeggios arranged as three-notes per string.

In the following diagrams, the white notes are played using a right-hand tap.

## C7 Arpeggio (3-notes-per-string)

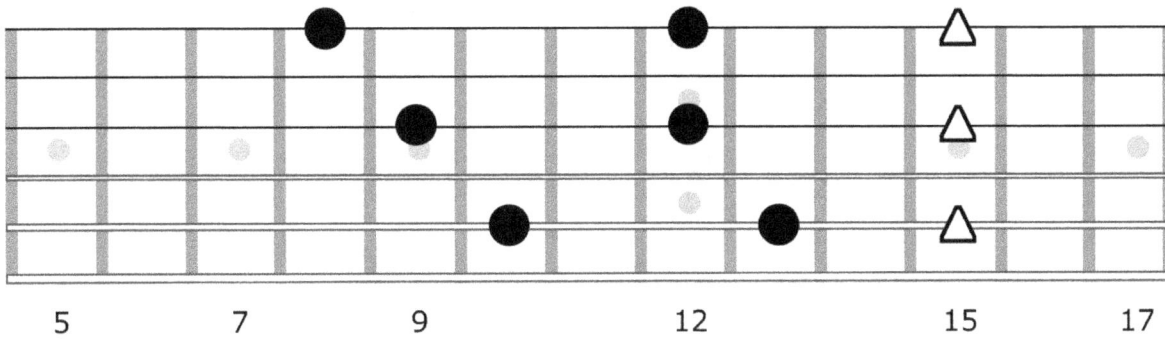

We can also play pentatonic scales arranged with four-notes per string.

## A Minor Pentatonic scale (4-notes-per-string)

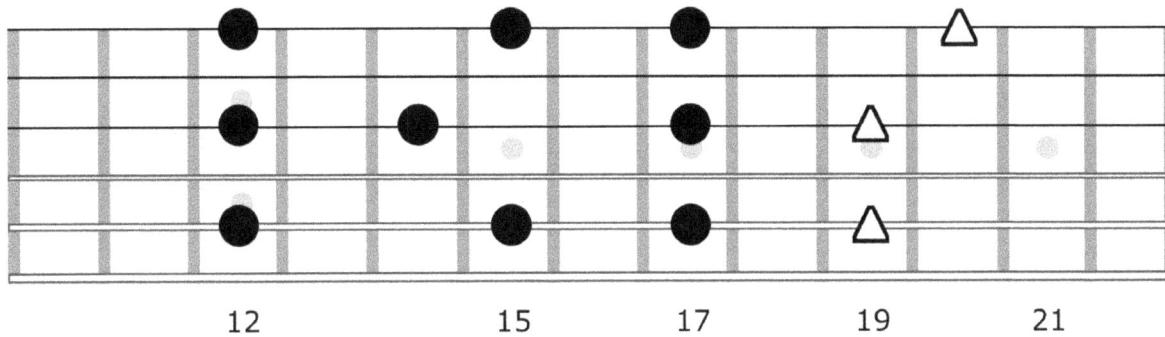

In No Picking Allowed-2, you'll see right from the start that some of the arpeggios switch early in anticipation of the subsequent chord. This gives the music a sense of urgency, and any tension created at the end of the bar is resolved with the arrival of the resolution chord in the bar that follows it.

## Bars 1-8

The first eight bars of the piece contain string-skipped arpeggios arranged with three notes per string. Since each note follows a logical four-note sequence, the arpeggios sound smooth and fluid, as if picked at hyper speed, rather than sounding like tapped notes.

Try using the first and third fingers of your fretting hand throughout, regardless of the fret spacing. This approach will be more consistent as you're using the same fingers the whole time, and it will produce a cleaner sound by allowing your fingers to lie flatter on the fretboard while damping any idle treble strings. Keep a decent gap between your first and second fingers to prevent them from sticking together.

**Photo 11a**

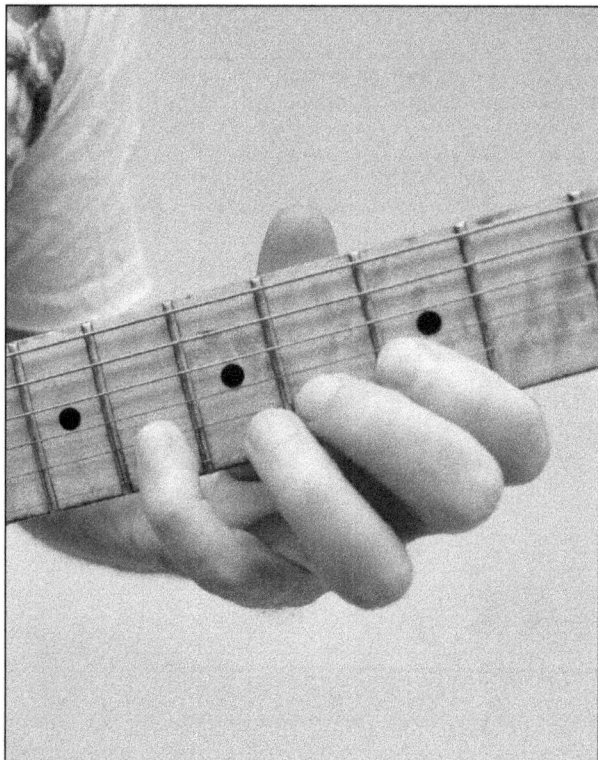

**Photo 11b**

Using tapping to play three-notes-per-string arpeggios like this allows for articulation at speeds that would be nearly impossible using traditional shapes.

**Bars 9-16**

These bars follow a more traditional approach to right-hand tapping, with occasional descents to the B string using left-hand tapping. Be careful to avoid sudden large shifts with the right hand as this can cause noticeable handling noise. After finishing each tap, begin shifting the right hand in a smooth, continuous movement.

Although much of this passage appears scalar, a closer analysis reveals that chord tones are targeted throughout.

**Bars 17-16**

The piece ends with a descending four-note arpeggio sequence (using A Minor and Bb Major) before leading to an ascending string-skipped Am arpeggio.

## No Picking Allowed-2

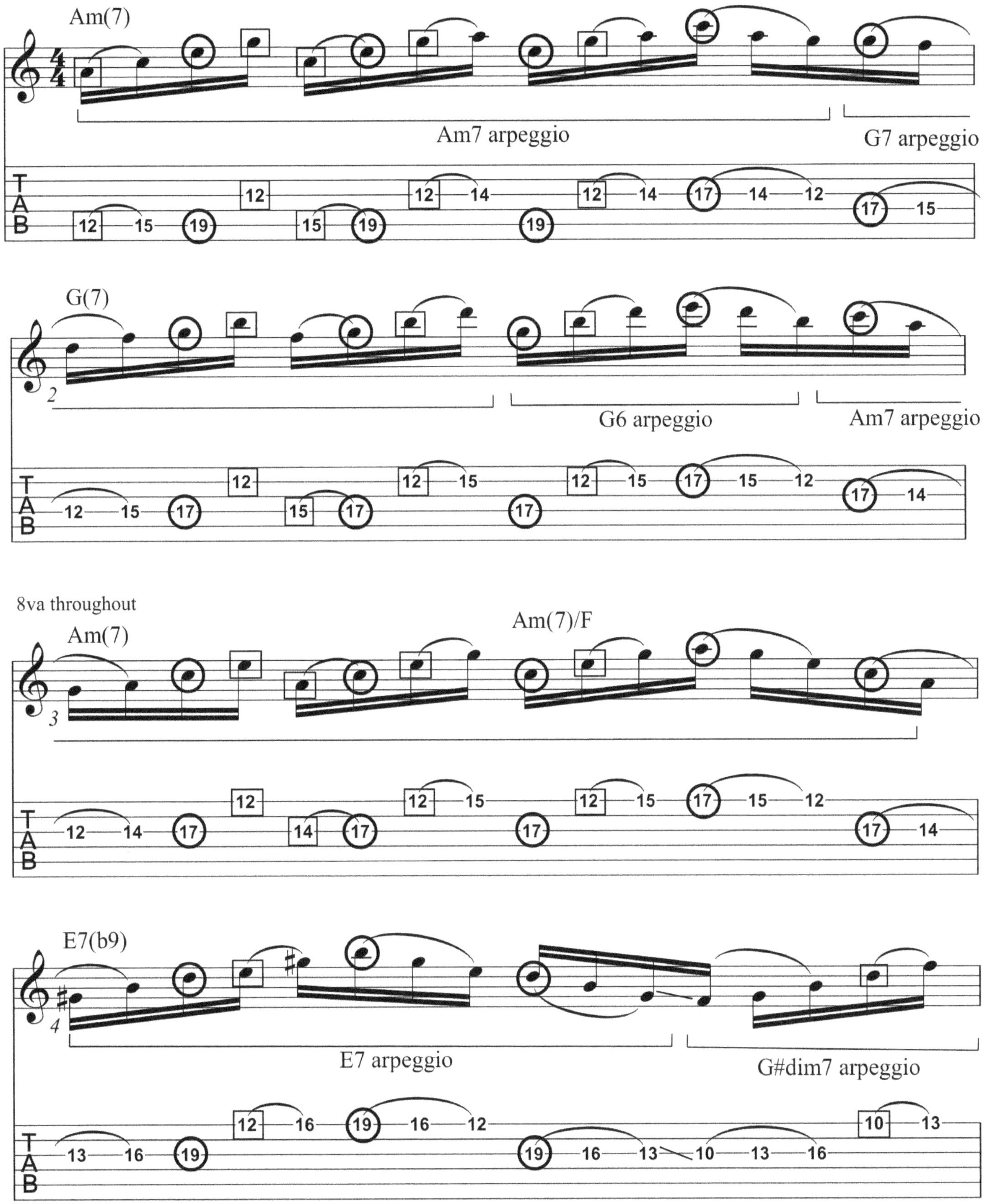

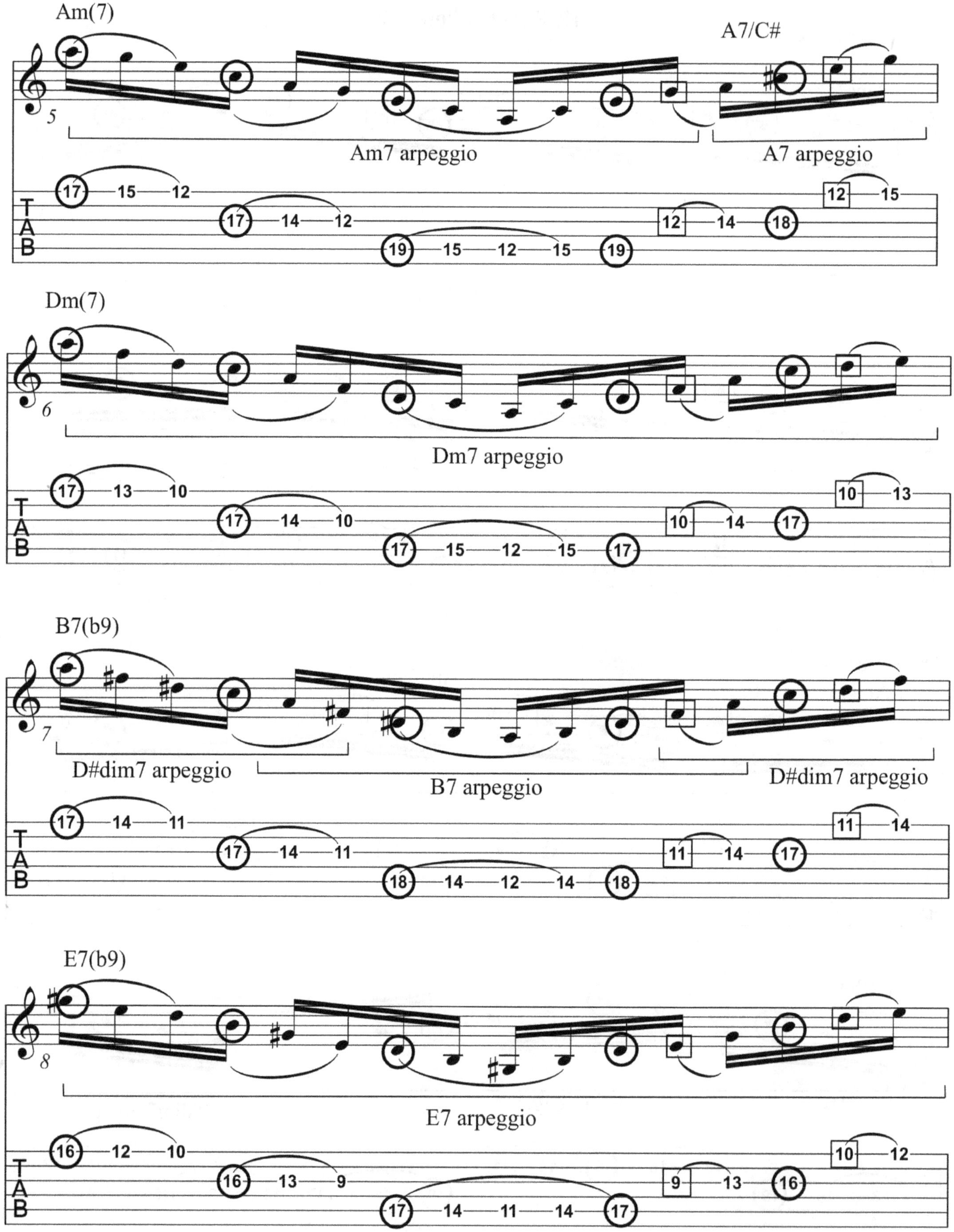
Am(7)
A7/C#
Am7 arpeggio
A7 arpeggio
Dm(7)
Dm7 arpeggio
B7(b9)
D#dim7 arpeggio
B7 arpeggio
D#dim7 arpeggio
E7(b9)
E7 arpeggio

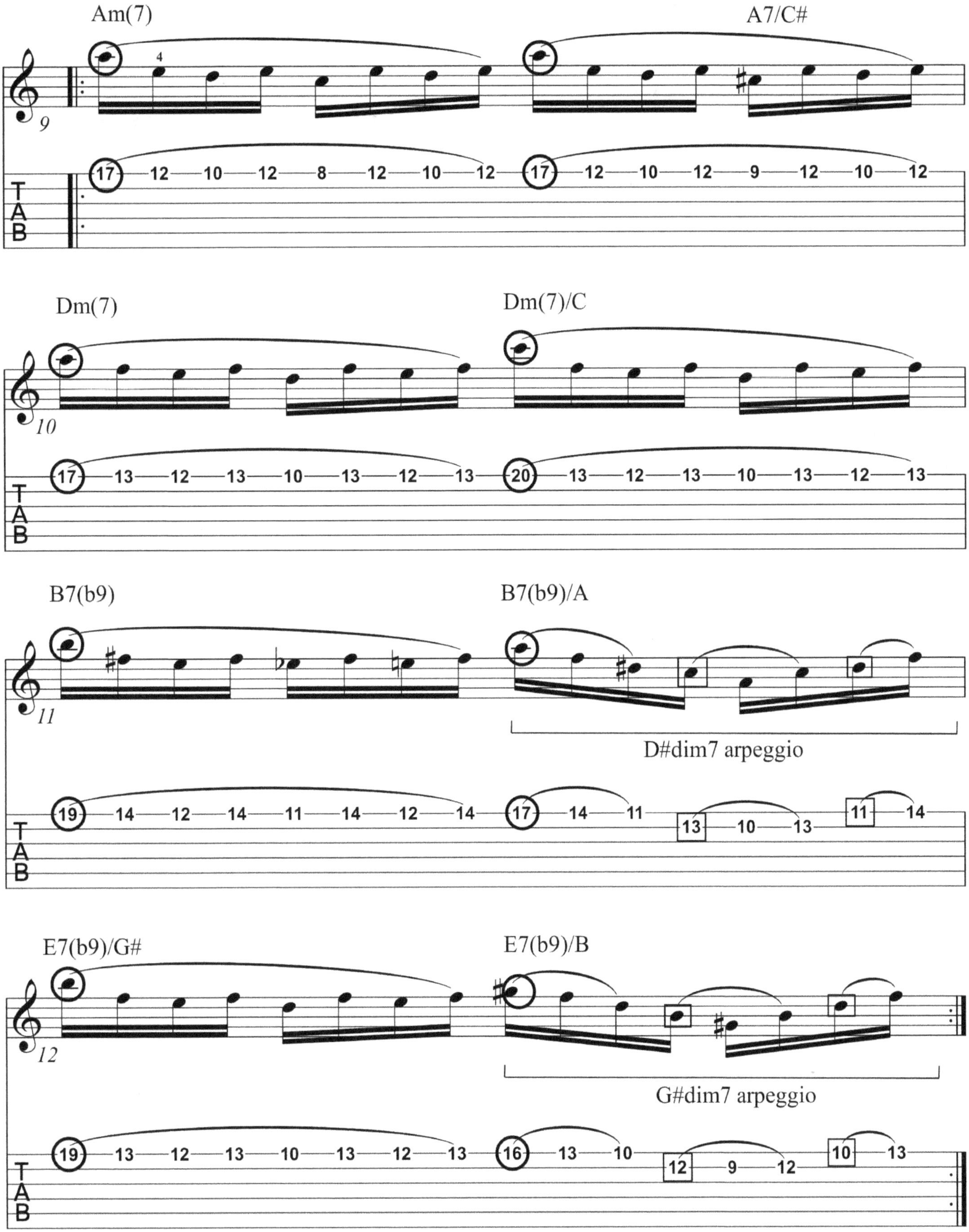
Am(7)
A7/C#
Dm(7)
Dm(7)/C
B7(b9)
B7(b9)/A
D#dim7 arpeggio
E7(b9)/G#
E7(b9)/B
G#dim7 arpeggio

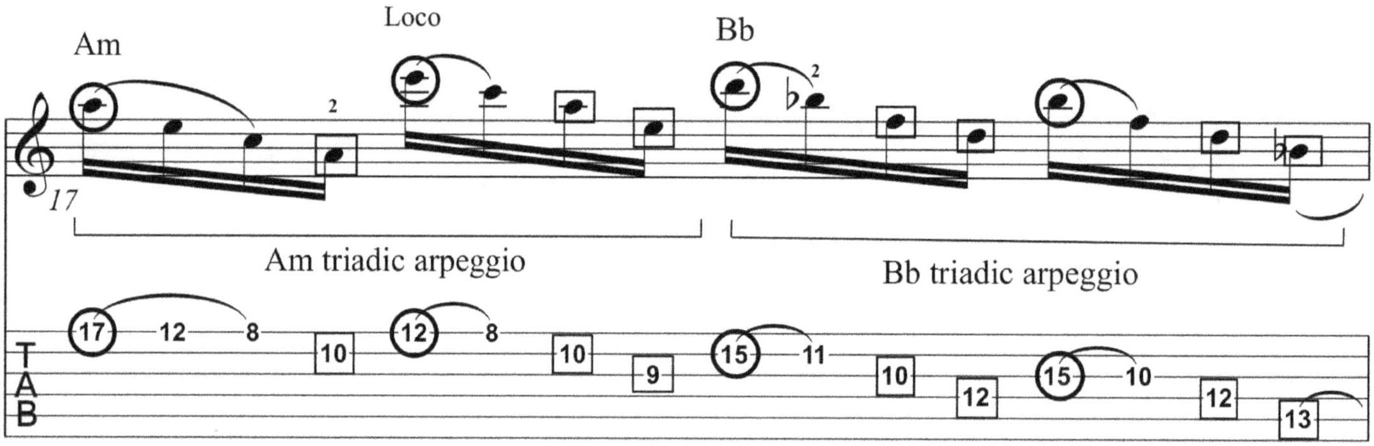
Loco
Am
Bb
Am triadic arpeggio
Bb triadic arpeggio

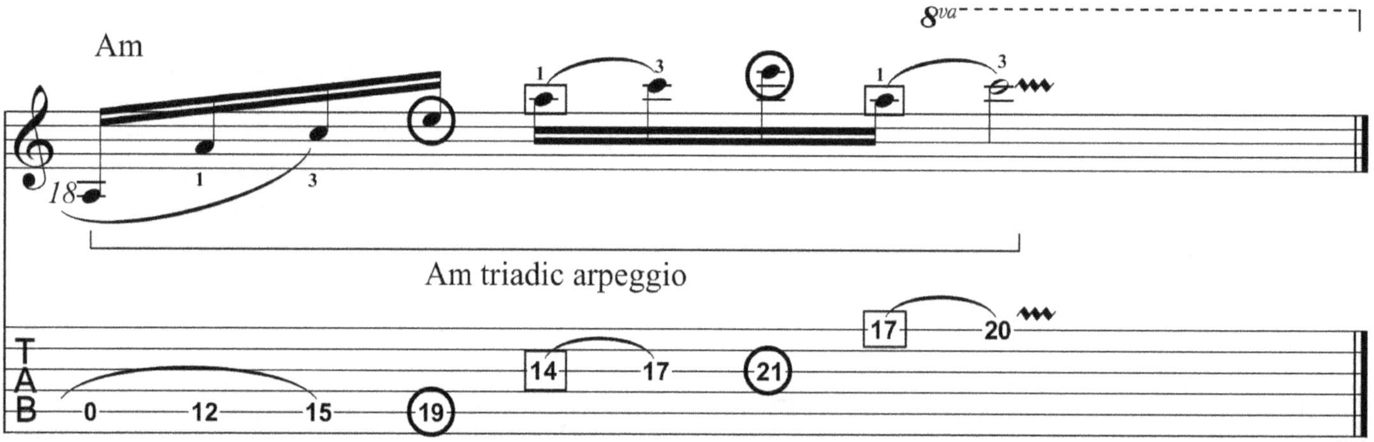
8va
Am
Am triadic arpeggio

# Chapter Seven: Right- and Left-hand Tapping Etudes Featuring Mixed Rhythms

## "Tap Dance"

This etude includes various musical approaches, such as blending different rhythms, slides with both hands, nested tuplets using right-hand tapping, double taps, applying taps to bends, and moving small structures along the neck.

The chord progression and backing track for this etude are also used in the next piece, Don't Faucet.

Technically, the recorded tempo is 80bpm, but I've written both pieces as though the tempo is 160bpm to prevent you from having to read a daunting array of thirty-second notes and thirty-second note triplets.

### Bars 1-4

In this first section, you'll play a melody using a tapped note on the 21st fret of the G string, combined with ascending and descending slides using the first finger of the fretting hand on the same string.

It ends with a left-hand tap on the 17th fret.

### Bar 5

This bar features more slides from the fretting hand. It's relatively easy to play this as each string starts with a right-hand tap. However, ensure that the pull-off from each right-hand tap is strong enough to clearly articulate the note at the beginning of each slide.

### Bar 6

In this section, the melody is played on a single string using a combination of tapping and slides with both the fretting and picking hands. While this melody could be played using conventional techniques, incorporating tapping and slides adds a unique, fluid quality to the sound.

### Bars 7-8

Here we combine right- and left-hand taps. Focus on lifting the left-hand tapping finger high enough off the fretboard so that it can come down onto the next string with enough strength to produce a clear note.

### Bars 9-10

Next, we have a series of right-hand assisted trills shifting up the neck. Each time the left-hand finger is lifted, a right-hand tap takes its place. Additionally, both fingers play a pull-off as they leave the fretboard, creating the effect of an impossibly fast trill.

The rhythm may look unusual on the page, but focus on maintaining a steady 1/4 note triplet rhythm with the right-hand taps and everything should fall into place.

### Bars 11-12

Here, the melody is outlined using "double taps" with the picking hand while the fretting hand remains on the same two frets, acting as a pedal point.

**Bars 13-14**

Tapping allows for a wide range of articulation. In this section of the study, bends and slides using both hands are featured, reminiscent of Eddie Van Halen's ground-breaking approach.

When bending, remember that the left hand provides the strength to hold the string up. Since the bends are foundational to this section, if they aren't accurate the rest of the passage will also be out of tune.

The transcription shows the specific frets being tapped by the right hand. However, the pitch produced will often be a tone higher than usual because much of the activity occurs on a string that is bent up a tone.

Finally, because holding a bend pushes the strings closer together, it is advantageous to pull off from each right-hand tap downwards in bar 14 to stop the tapping finger crashing into other strings.

**Bars 15-16**

This section combines slides using both hands, but like bar five it's relatively easy to play, as each new string begins with a right-hand tap. It also features consecutive slides with the first finger.

**Bars 17-19**

This passage uses right-hand taps on the D string to allow a left-hand tap with the first finger on the G string, creating a pathway that resembles the top of a castle wall.

Be careful with timing in this section, as the melody might tempt you to emphasise the wrong notes. Stay aware of which notes land on the start of each beat (group of four 1/16th notes), and practice targeting them to align with the 1/4 note pulse.

# Tap Dance

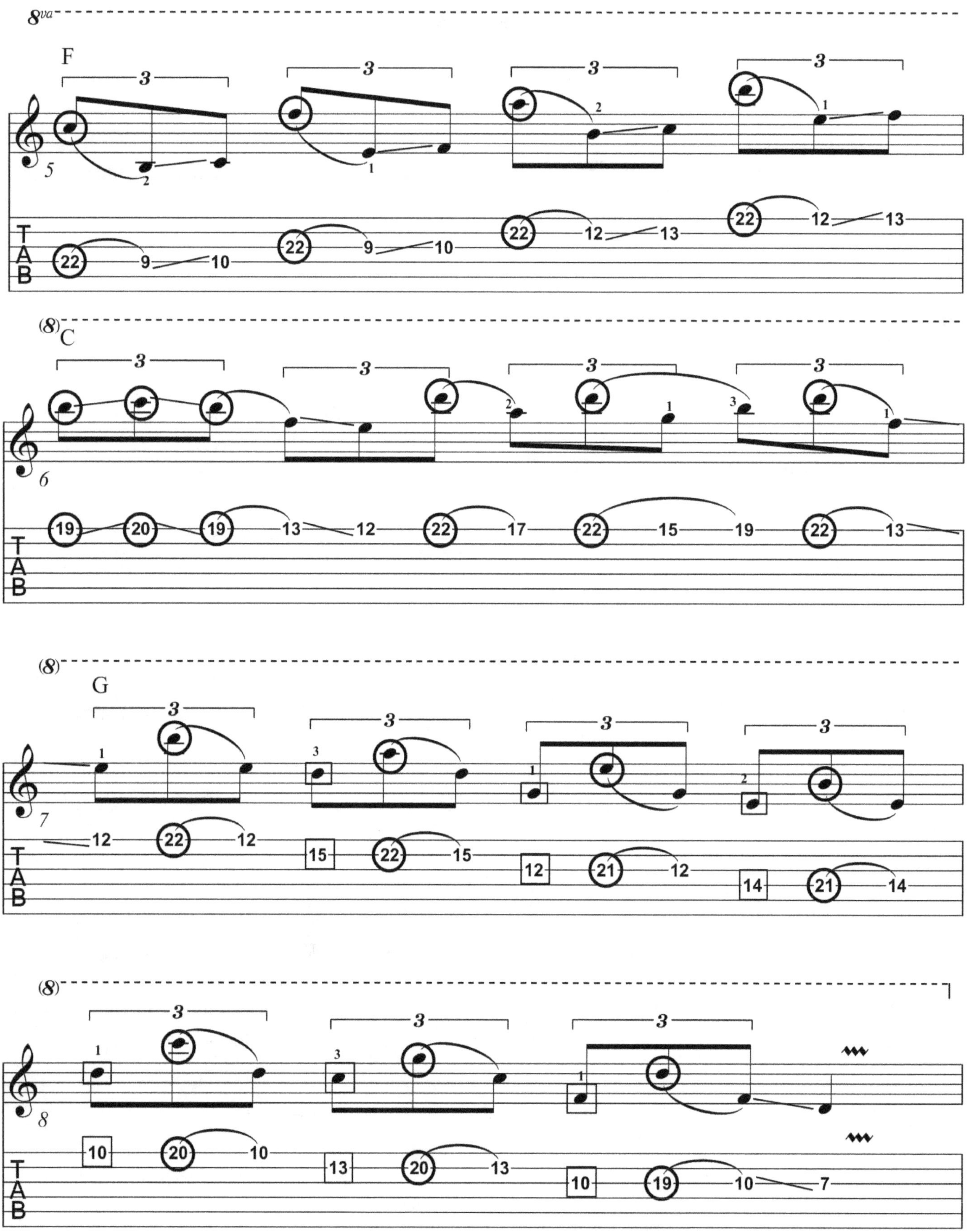
8va
F
C
G
T
A
B

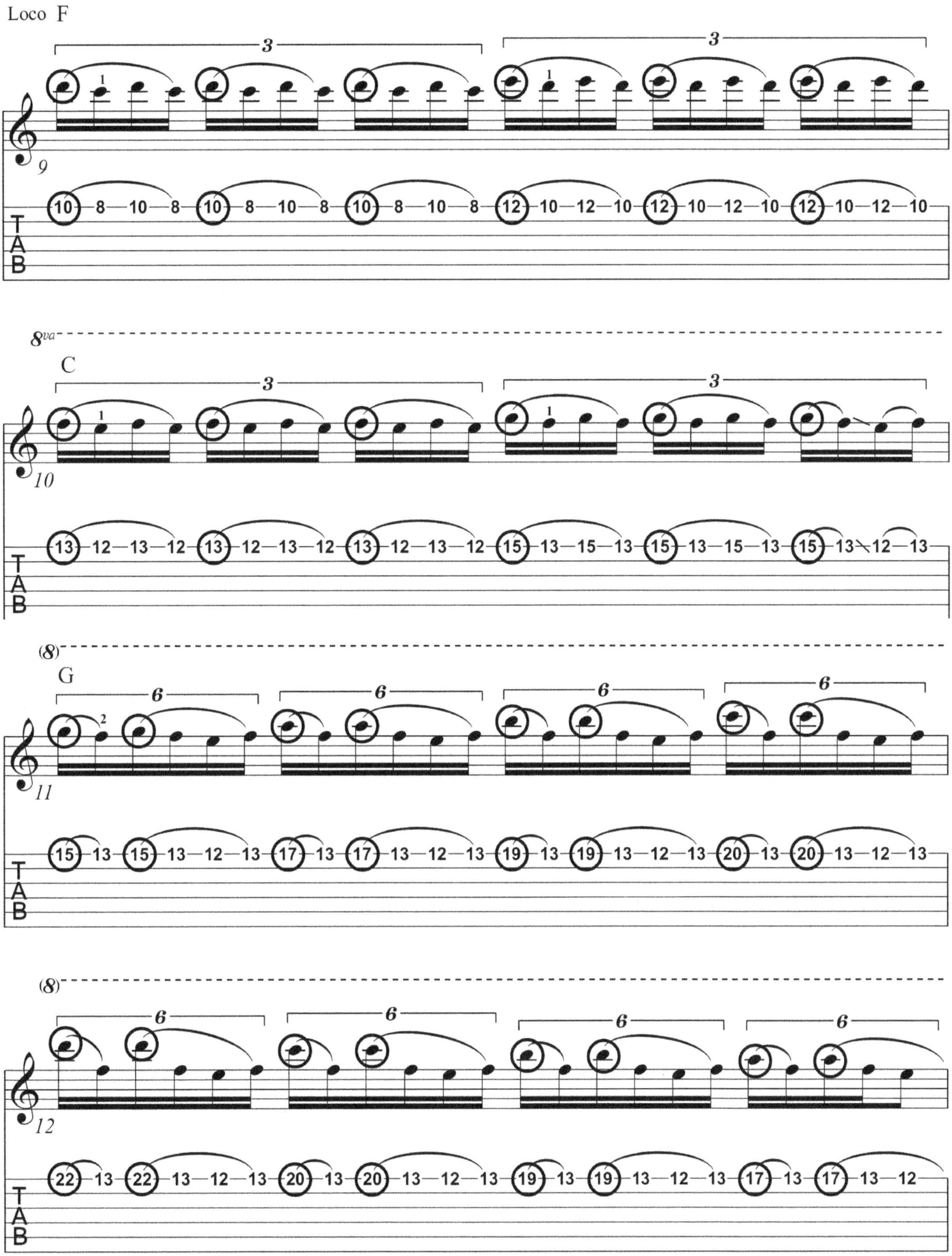
Loco F
3
8va
C
(8)
G
6
(8)
TAB

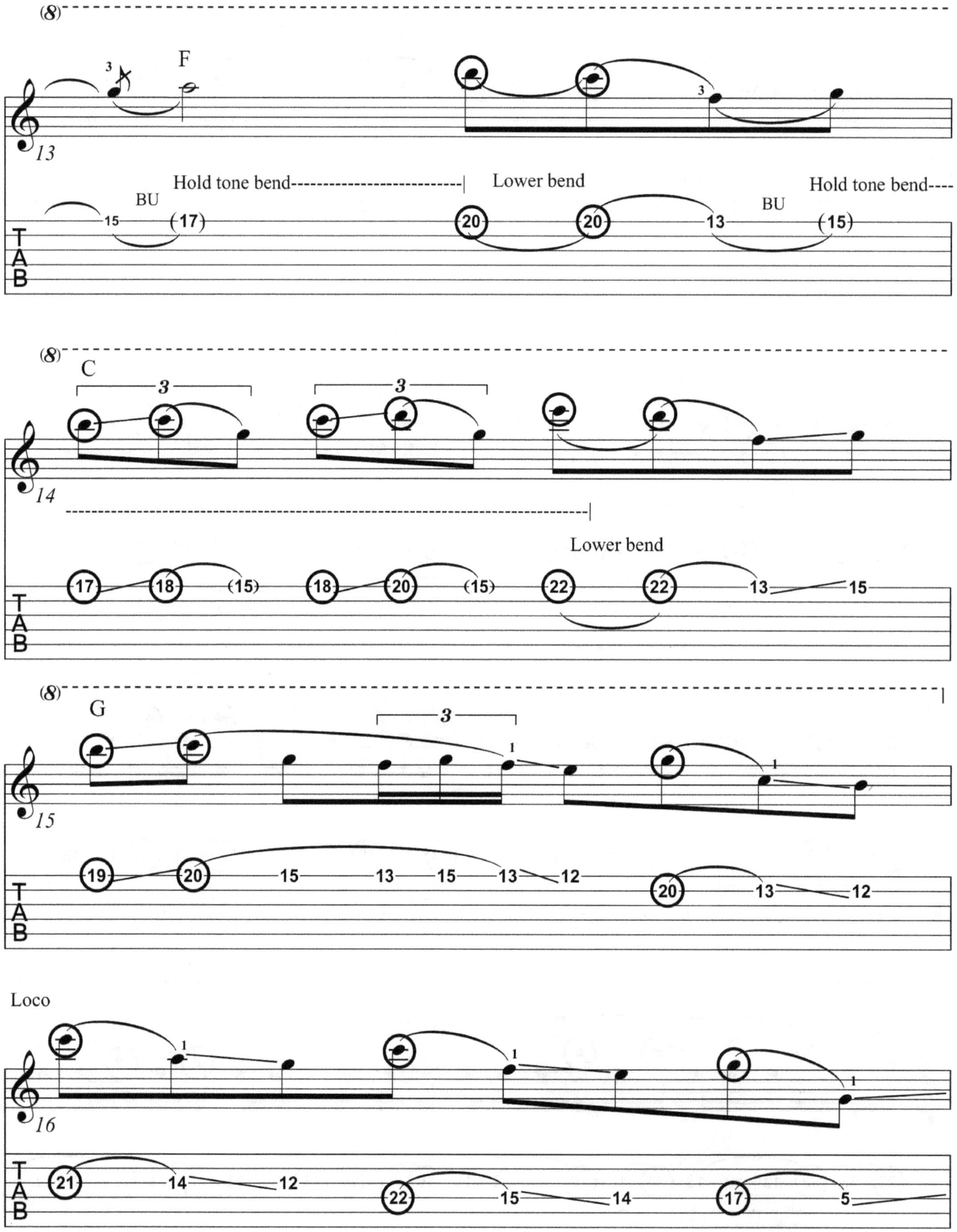
(8)
F
Hold tone bend
Lower bend
Hold tone bend
BU
BU
C
Lower bend
G
Loco

G(7)

gliss

sl

```
T       7   9  (10)  [7]  9  (10)  9   7  9  10  (12)  10   9      (12)  10   9
A
B
```

C

```
T      10  12  (14)  [10]  12  (14)  12  10  12  14  (16)  14  12   (15)  14  12  14
A
B
```
*18*         *19*

## "Don't Faucet"

This etude incorporates more left-hand tapping and contains a variety of musical approaches in different rhythms. These include quintuplets mixed with sextuplets, string skips, first-finger left-hand taps, lateral motion of large structures, and more. It uses the same chord sequence and backing track as Tap Dance.

**Bars 0-2**

The opening section features more Van Halen-style tapped bends. Again, remember that the left hand is responsible for providing the strength for both bending and vibrato. As with the previous solo, if any of your bends are out of tune, the taps added to that bend will also sound out of tune.

Finally, because we are adding taps to bends, remember to pull off downwards from each right-hand tap to stop the tapping finger crashing into other strings. Note the same approach should also be applied in bars 13-14.

**Bars 3-4**

This section is designed to strengthen your left-hand taps with the first finger. Note how right-hand taps are used at the end of this and the following bar to allow time for the large left-hand position shifts.

**Bars 5-6**

These two bars feature a technique where a note is repeated by alternating between a right-hand tap and a left-hand slide. Ensure there's a strong pull-off from the right-hand tap so the left-hand slide sounds strong and clear.

## Bars 7-8

Here, the two right-hand-tapped notes on each string could be played using two fingers of the right hand, but using a slide with one finger will sound more distinct and vocal.

## Bars 9-10

The straight 1/16th note descending pattern in these two bars is easy to play but surprisingly effective.

## Bars 11-12

Now we have a descending three-note scale sequence where the first note of each beat is an octave higher than the second. This adds a glitter to the sequence and is a technique I refer to as *mirror tapping*, as it involves mirroring the left hand with right-hand taps an octave higher.

## Bars 13-14

Eddie Van Halen introduced tapping to the mainstream and bar thirteen demonstrates a typical approach he used. He often played a series of bends by sliding the tapping hand to different notes along one string, while the left hand bent the same string from behind (in this case, at the 5th fret of the G string). As usual, the vibrato in bar fourteen is applied to the tap using the left hand.

## Bars 15-19

The solo study finishes with an ascending sequence that alternates between quintuplets and 1/16th note triplets. This may seem challenging, but focus on the notes at the start of each beat (the taps on the E string and the notes slid on the B string) and everything should fall into place.

Try using only the first two fingers of your fretting hand throughout this final section. You'll find it stronger and more consistent.

# Don't Faucet

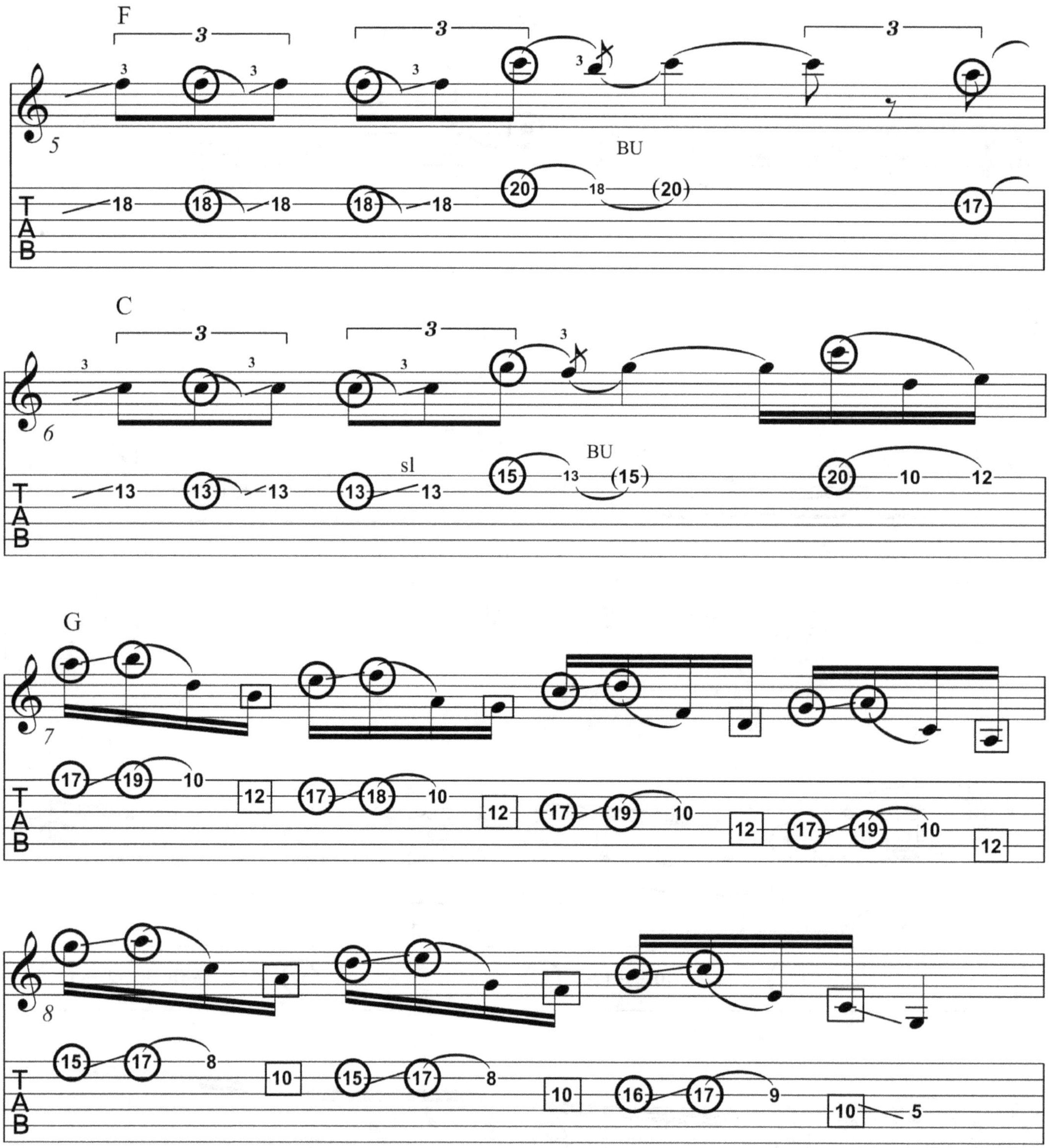
F
BU
C
sl
BU
G

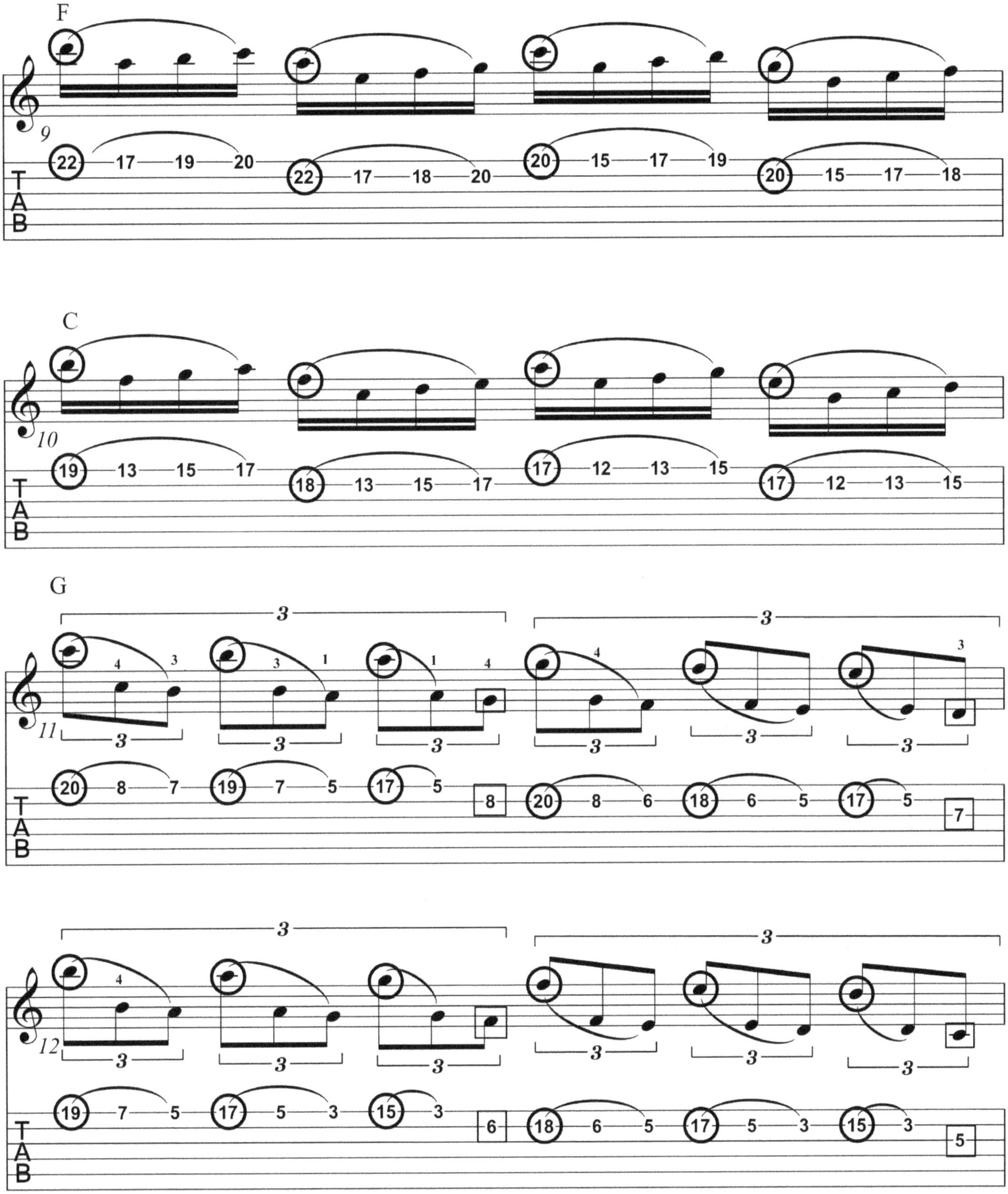
F
22 17 19 20 22 17 18 20 20 15 17 19 20 15 17 18
C
19 13 15 17 18 13 15 17 17 12 13 15 17 12 13 15
G
20 8 7 19 7 5 17 5 8 20 8 6 18 6 5 17 5 7
19 7 5 17 5 3 15 3 6 18 6 5 17 5 3 15 3 5

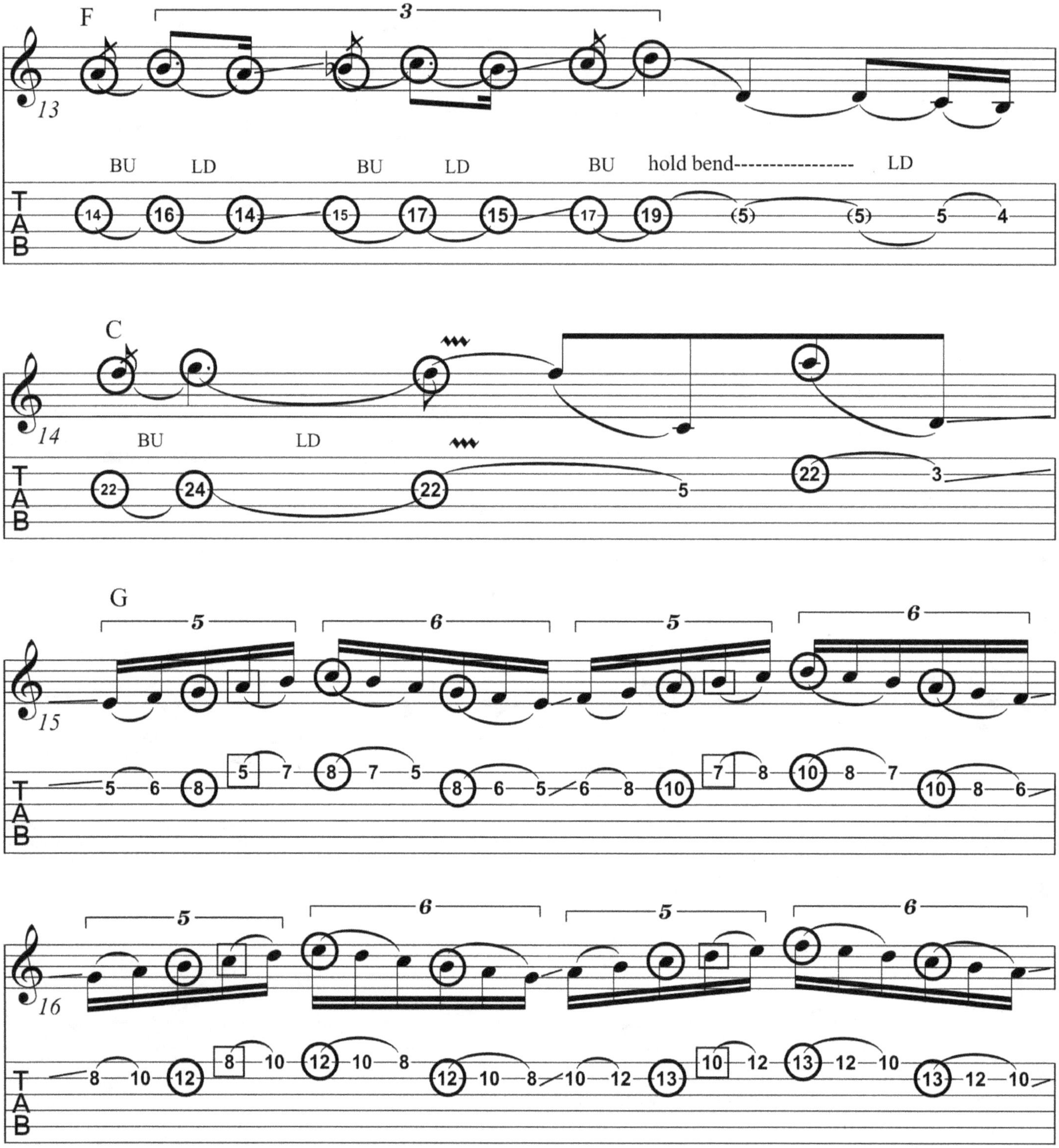
F
BU
LD
BU
LD
BU
hold bend-----------------
LD
C
BU
LD
G

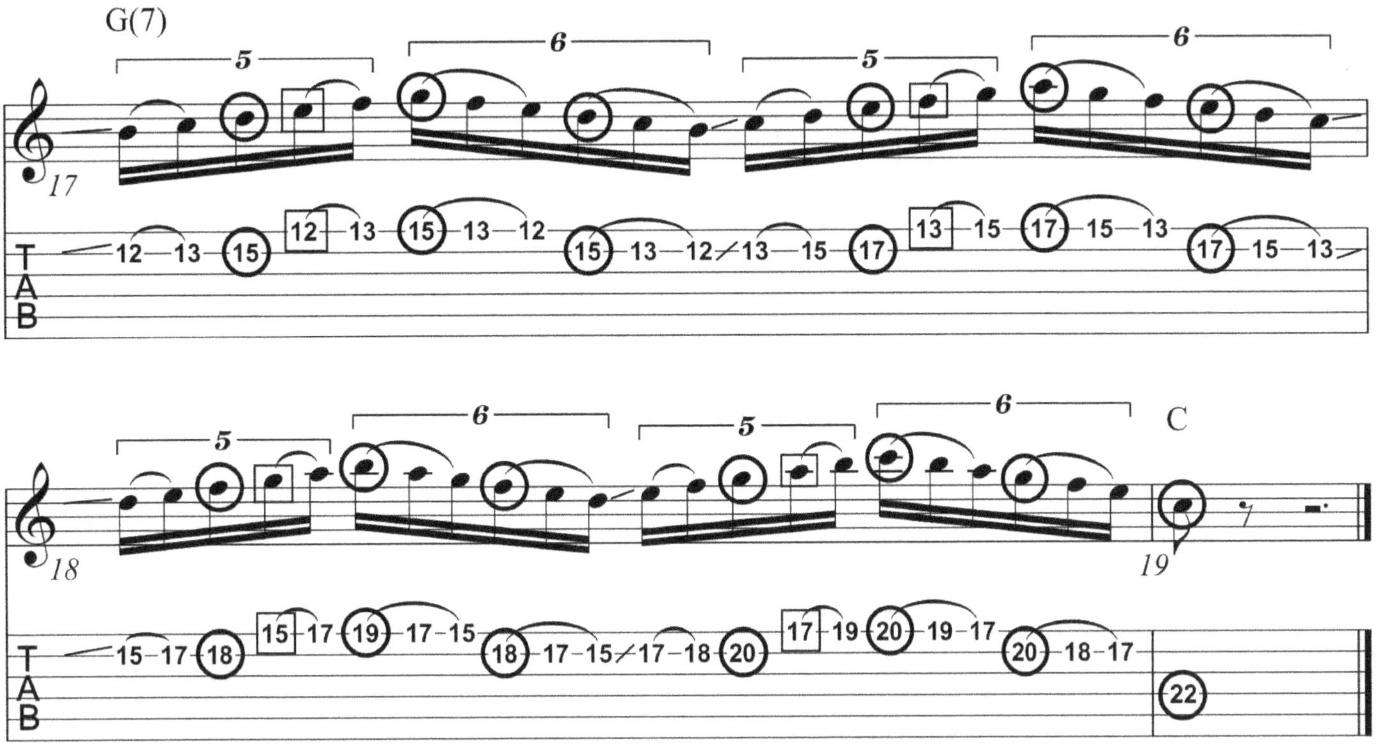
G(7)
C

# Chapter Eight: Combining Various Legato and Tapping Techniques

### "Aye Aye Skipper"

We wrap things up with a short and sweet section that incorporates all the techniques we've covered.

**Bars 1-4**

This first section has a neo-classical feel and is picked to provide a contrast to the legato-based sections that follow. Notice how the string skips create a sense of melodic counterpoint between the notes on different strings.

**Bars 5-6**

Here, the 1/16th note feel of this passage contrasts with the 1/8th note triplet feel of the previous four bars. There are several ways to pick this passage, one of which could be hybrid picking. If you find the left-hand taps in the transcription difficult, try experimenting with other picking methods to find what works best for you. I find that the left-hand taps make it much easier for my picking hand.

**Bars 7-8**

In both bars, the notes on the G string create a rhythmic counterpoint to the notes on the top E string, with the band playing rhythmic stabs to mirror this rhythm. Each note on the G string is marked with a hairpin accent, and I chose to pick these notes to give them more punch.

**Bars 9-10**

In this symmetrical passage of 4ths and octaves, the four-note melodic figure on each beat gains depth through string skips, covering a wide range with just a few notes.

Instead of relying on the left-hand taps shown in the transcription, you could explore other techniques like hybrid picking. For instance, to hybrid-pick the first two beats of bar nine (the first eight notes), you could use an upstroke with your ring finger for the high string, an upstroke with your middle finger for the G string, and your pick to pluck the first note on the A string with a downstroke.

**Bars 11-13**

The piece concludes with some straightforward four-notes-per-string scale patterns using left- and right-hand tapping.

The rhythms in these last two bars may appear complicated, but there's a reason for writing them this way. With 24 evenly spaced notes in each bar, everything could technically be written as 1/16th note triplets. However, this would cause the taps to fall on different stress points each time.

Instead, by following the rhythm in the transcription, the first note on each string (played using a left-hand tap) aligns with a simple 1/4 note triplet pulse. This 1/4 note triplet pulse better reflects the thought process of a player in a passage like this – rather than focusing on 1/16th note triplets, which have four pulses per bar instead of six.

# Aye Aye Skipper

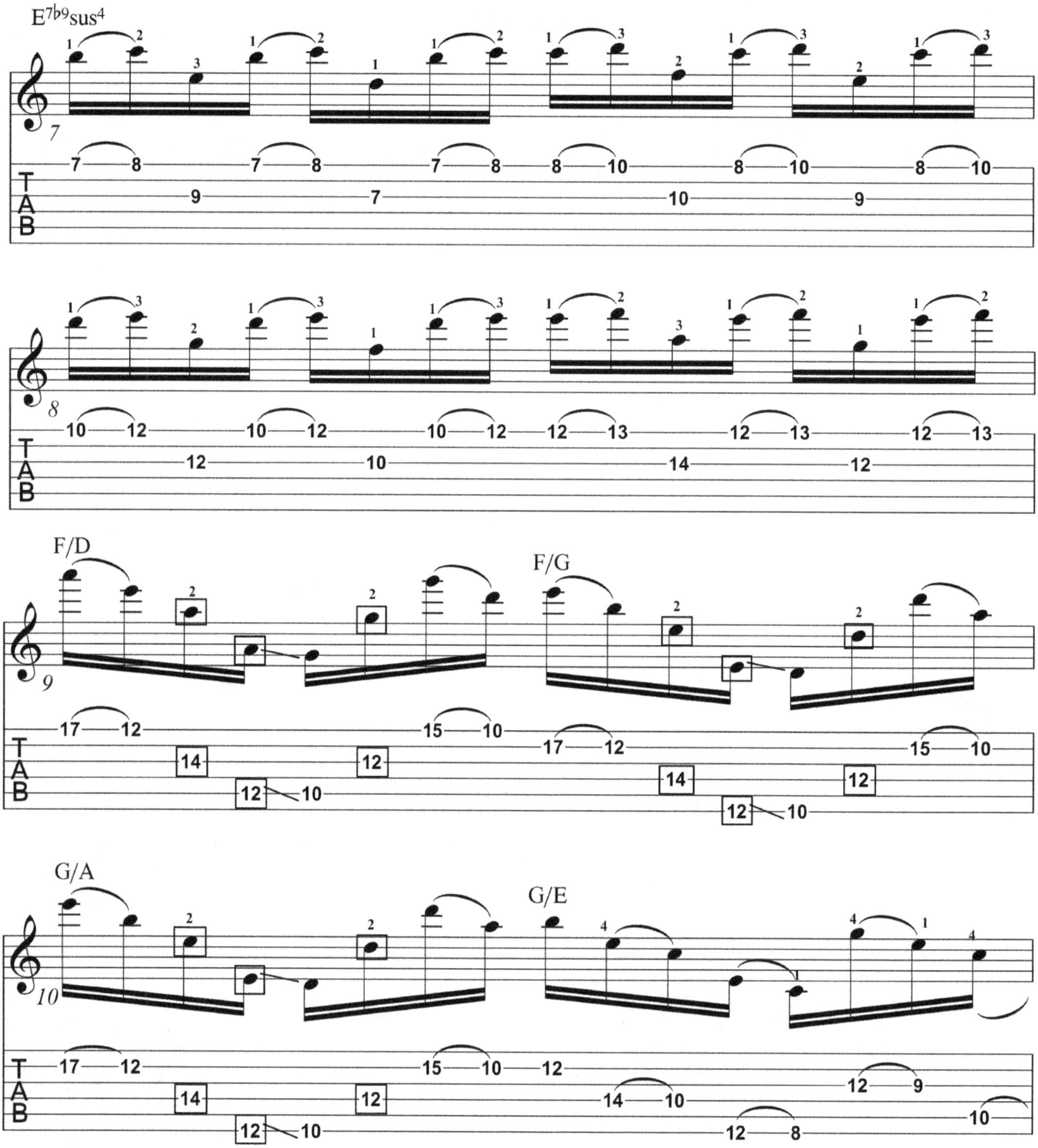
E7♭9sus4
F/D
F/G
G/A
G/E

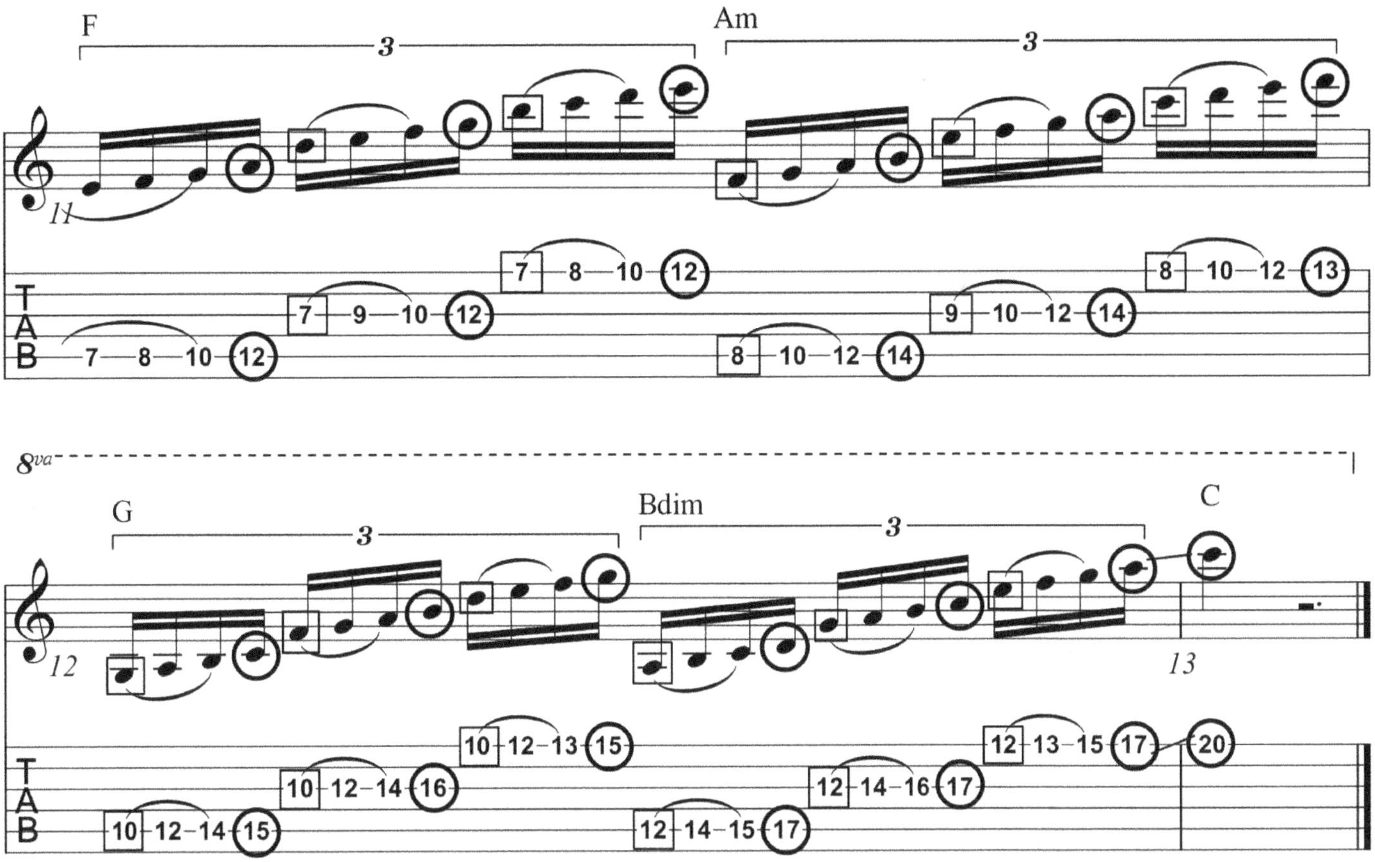
F
Am
11
8va
G
Bdim
C
12
13

# Conclusion

I hope this book has helped you see your playing in a new light, allowing you to view legato as more than just a way to play fast. Instead, you can now appreciate it for the fluid tone it creates.

You now have the choice of playing with attack (picking) or without attack (legato), depending on what sounds best for the situation. Players like Greg Howe often go to great lengths to give their runs and licks a more keyboard-like quality by relying heavily on hammer-ons and pull-offs. While this approach can make the fingerings more challenging, many players find it worth the effort for the smooth, attractive tone it produces.

## Technical Balance

Even though this book has focused solely on legato, in most musical situations, legato will form just a component of your overall approach.

When playing in Carl Palmer's band (in which I had to play all Keith Emerson's keyboard parts on guitar), I would usually select between two binary choices when faced with a tricky melody:

- Picking every note

- Picking only the first note on each string

However, sometimes, I was unhappy with the results of both approaches. It was either difficult to play and/or didn't sound quite right.

After a while, I realised that the solution was neither of the above. The best results often came from using a combination of the two, which involved picking every note except the last one on each string.

Most players can pick quite quickly on a single string – it's changing from one string to another that poses the problem. Consequently, many players, such as John Scofield, Scott Henderson and Josh Meader, apply a simple rule: where there is more than one note on a string, don't pick the last note on that string.

Playing the last note on a string using a hammer-on or pull-off buys time for the picking hand to get into position to start picking the subsequent string.

This labour-saving approach (which I usually refer to as "half & half") takes the pressure off both hands. Compared to the binary choice/dilemma described earlier, this approach involves less work for the picking hand than when picking everything, and far less work for the fretting hand than when only picking the first note on each string.

Jazz guitarists Jim Hall and Allan Holdsworth have both compared picking everything as the equivalent of a saxophonist tonguing every note. They prefer a mixture of articulation so that it sounds less rigid and more natural.

The half & half approach offers the best of both worlds, as it sounds like tight legato or incredibly smooth picking.

Example 9a demonstrates the half & half principle in action. While this approach is technically easier over time, very few players find it natural at first. Most either try to pick everything or stick to legato by picking only the first note on each string. If you want to explore this method, you'll need to consistently apply the "don't pick the last note on each string" rule until it becomes second nature.

Finally, although economy picking is shown here, there's so little pressure on the picking hand that you'll have the freedom to use any stroke you prefer. Plus, all the legato practice you've done in this book will make those parts feel effortless.

**Example 9a**

## Suggested Listening

The late Allan Holdsworth is widely regarded as the pioneer and master of legato playing, and his music shows what's possible using just left-hand legato.

When it comes to combining left- and right-hand tapping, Scott Mishoe achieves spectacular effects, even though he typically uses only one finger for right-hand taps.

For eight-finger tapping, two players come to mind who use this approach exclusively: fusion guitarist T.J. Helmerich (with distortion) and jazz guitarist Stanley Jordan (clean).

## String Dampers

Controlling noise is a key challenge when using legato techniques, so you might consider following players like Matteo Mancuso by using a string damper – either a hair tie or a professional clamp that attaches to the fretboard near the nut. However, keep in mind that this will prevent you from using open strings and pure harmonics. It might be worth persevering and refining your technique to play cleanly without relying on such devices.

## Limitation Leads to Fluency

Practicing one specific aspect of playing for an extended period is a great way to dig deeper into your creative resources. It helps you to avoid relying on obvious patterns each time you use a certain technique.

To become fluent with legato, aim to build a vocabulary that lets you move freely around the guitar using right-hand tapping alongside left-hand legato. For example, see how long you can keep things interesting on just one string. There are many possibilities to explore, such as adding slides or pick-scrapes with the right hand, and slides, bends, or vibrato with the left. Remember, any vibrato on a right-hand-tapped note should be produced by the left hand lower on the same string.

Above all, focus on creating music that is expressive, not just mechanically proficient.

Good luck, and happy practicing!

*Shaun*